Praise for ACCOUNT PLANNING *in* SALESFORCE

Donal uncovers the vast advantages of Account Planning done right and shows how our own client intimacy approach has benefitted from getting closer to our customers.

Patricia Elizondo, Senior Vice President, **Xerox Corporation**

Companies around the globe are transforming the way they connect with customers. **ACCOUNT PLANNING *in* SALESFORCE** contains valuable advice on how to use Account Planning methodology in Salesforce to accelerate revenue growth. It is a great example of how our partners are leveraging the power of the Salesforce platform to provide customers with the right tools to accelerate their success in the cloud.

Ron Huddleston, Senior Vice President, ISV & Channel, **salesforce.com**

Unlike most books on this topic, Donal grounds his recommendations in the context of modern B2B sales, where customers – armed with massive amounts of information and advice – can afford to engage salespeople later and later in the purchase decision. In this world, an insight-based approach must serve as the backbone of a powerful Account Plan. And, as Donal demonstrates, there are no shortcuts to getting this right. This book is required reading for those of us who want to keep selling and avoid the trap of order-taking.

Matthew Dixon, Executive Director Sales & Service Practice, **CEB** and co-author of *The Challenger Sale*

Even a dyslexic, A.D.D., former CEO like me found it to be a compelling relevant read … Love the statistical back up … Practical and relevant … I've turned around over a dozen sales teams in my career and the content provided in this book is the basis for that success. Daly nailed it!

Ken Bado, former CEO, **Marklogic** and EVP, **Autodesk**

A must-read for all sales professionals working in a salesforce.com environment! Account Planning is a core sales skill that requires a disciplined approach and ongoing care and maintenance. The book not only teaches the 'how,' but 'why' proper Account Planning will drive bigger and stronger sales opportunities.

Matthew L. Cox, Senior Director, Sales Strategy and Operations, **Hewlett-Packard**

All too often Account Planning is a once-a-year effort that gathers dust on the shelf. Use Donal Daly's **ACCOUNT PLANNING** *in* **SALESFORCE** to help transform this critical activity into a usable, customer-centric approach to growing loyal relationships all year long.

Bob Thompson, Founder / CEO, **CustomerThink Corp.**

Donal's unique combination of methodology expertise and smart software comes to life in this book. It is filled with priceless nuggets. If you want to operationalize Account Planning, this is the best roadmap I've seen. I encourage all sales professionals to follow it.

Carol Burch, former Global SVP, CRM Clear Vision Program, **SAP**

A practical guide that embraces the modern world of global Account Management with a refreshing balance of integrity, knowledge, expertise, and humor. Daly's business acumen is evident as he clearly articulates what it takes to maximize revenue from Large Accounts. A must read and, dare I say it, an enjoyable read …

Padma Rao, Director Sales Enablement, **Akamai**

This book is a no-brainer for sales reps and sales executives who want to maximize revenue from large accounts. It's filled with practical strategies you can implement right away.

Jill Konrath, author of *SNAP Selling* and *Selling to Big Companies*

Account planning must live and breathe as part of how you run your business. It needs to become part of your culture, and should be integrated into your overall business cadence. If you want to drive the right culture and cadence for Account Planning in your business, this book is a blueprint to start with.

Peter Jofriet, Director, Sales Excellence, **Honeywell Process Solutions**

ACCOUNT PLANNING *in* **SALESFORCE** helps companies focus and collaborate on creating value for critical accounts, and Dealmaker Smart Account Manager is a critical component. We are excited to add the combination of the book and the software to the portfolio of sales enablement tools we support. If you use salesforce.com you should definitely read this book!

Walter Rogers, CEO, **CloudCoaching International**

This is the only Account Management book I've seen that effectively maps methodology with technology, a critical weapon in the armory of today's sales professional.

Gerhard Gschwandtner, CEO, **Selling Power**

While many authors only address one or the other, in this book Donal has addressed the intersection of both technology and methodology, the necessary mix of pragmatic principles of Account Planning coupled with the operation of CRM. The book brilliantly covers both the 'what' and the 'how to.' Whether you use Salesforce or any other CRM system, if you want to master Account Planning and maximize your personal performance, this book is a must read!

David Brock, President, **Partners in Excellence**

ACCOUNT PLANNING *in* **SALESFORCE** is a roadmap for successful Account Planning. Easy to read, full of crucial advice, it should be used by every Account Team selling to large customers. Strongly recommended.

Anne O'Leary, Executive Chairman, **Kinematik**

We all know that focusing on the right customers, and only the right customers, unlocks sales success. But how many of us put this into practice? This book holds the key to maximizing revenue from your biggest customers, and guides you through making it a repeatable practice by integrating it with Salesforce. Don't just read this book – use it as a playbook and then act!

York Baur, CEO, **Windermere Solutions**

Sales people often confuse Account Planning with just having multiple opportunities in the same Account. Donal has ably demonstrated that the greatest win lies not in individual opportunities but in getting the overall Account Strategy right. This book clearly lays out a systematic way of planning, executing and tracking that strategy by leveraging technology as a true enabler. In this easy-to-follow book, Donal shows how it can be done.

John Golden, President & CEO, **Huthwaite**

At Chasm Institute we've long promoted market development concepts that seem mirrored here in Donal's Account Planning methodologies. Stand-alone, they are best-of breed. Integrated as a native Salesforce application, they are killer. **ACCOUNT PLANNING** *in* **SALESFORCE** will not only teach you The TAS Group's methodologies … it is a practical, no-nonsense guide for leveraging your Salesforce investment. And, the classic rock music references are both amusing and useful!

Mark Cavender, founder & Managing Director, **Chasm Institute LLC**

The title of this book could have easily been **ACCOUNT EXECUTION**. In his book, Donal lays out a pragmatic approach that makes Account Plans actionable, leveraging the benefits of salesforce.com and providing a roadmap on how to harvest key client relationships for sustainable and repeatable revenue.

Jim Ninivaggi, Service Director, **SiriusDecisions**

Finally!!! ... a book that describes the best practices of Account Planning, and offers practical steps to use the most popular Salesforce support technology to implement. I love the section on trust! Account Managers and Teams should read the book, apply the concepts, and benefit from the increased revenue and improved Account relationships that will result.

David Roberts, Assistant Professor, Sales Discipline at Kenan-Flagler Business School at UNC

I have to believe Donal had a blast writing this rich, insightful, and utterly practical book. He toggles back and forth among his roles as engineer, CEO, and salesperson, expertly providing the reader with what they need to understand about Account Management – especially the fact that it isn't just a string of sales opportunities from the same customer, as many still think. This is an eye-opener and a must-read for anyone accountable for building long-term, mutually profitable relationships with key accounts.

Dave Stein, CEO & Founder, ES Research Group, Inc.

ACCOUNT PLANNING *in* SALESFORCE

UNLOCK REVENUE IN BIG CUSTOMERS TO TURN THEM INTO BIGGER CUSTOMERS

Donal Daly

Published by Oak Tree Press
19 Rutland Street, Cork, Ireland
www.oaktreepress.com

A catalogue record of this book is available from the British Library.

ISBN 978 1 78119 086 9 (Hardback)
ISBN 978 1 78119 087 6 (Paperback)
ISBN 978 1 78119 088 3 (ePub)
ISBN 978 1 78119 089 0 (Kindle)

CONTENTS

FIGURES

DEDICATION

To my father who passed away on November 17, 2012, and from whom I learned the value of perspective and the importance of a moral compass. He was an inspiration to me.

The profits from **ACCOUNT PLANNING IN SALESFORCE** will be donated to WITNESS, an international nonprofit organization that has been using the power of video and storytelling for 20 years to open the eyes of the world to human rights abuses. Co-founded by musician and human rights advocate Peter Gabriel, Human Rights First and the Reebok Human Rights Foundation, WITNESS empowers human rights defenders to use video to fight injustice, and to transform personal stories of abuse into powerful tools that can pressure those in power or with power to act.

The TAS Group has been a supporter of WITNESS since 2006. For more information about WITNESS, please go to **www.witness.org**.

INTRODUCTION

An undertaking like this book is beyond the capacity of the author alone. At each step along the way, I received extraordinary support and guidance from a broad constituency of contributors and reviewers.

At the core of the book is the Account Planning and Management methodology from The TAS Group, which owes its value to our customers across the globe, the many methodology experts who preceded me in earlier incarnations of The TAS Group, and my current colleagues. It is through their implementation experience that we have been able to refine the methodology, and the supporting tools and models that are incarnated in the Dealmaker software platform.

But deep gratitude is due to Marc Benioff, CEO of salesforce.com, and the visionaries who joined with him in foreseeing a new way of delivering business software applications. Before the term 'cloud-computing' was invented, these luminaries envisioned a solution for the business software user untrammeled by the constraints of traditional enterprise software, freed from the limitations of deskbound systems access, and empowered by a software application that could be accessed anywhere, anytime.

It was this exciting vision, and the re-imagining of enterprise software, coming to life in the early part of this century, that was the exemplar to me (and many others) to invent new ways of approaching traditional business problems. In our case, our Mount Everest was sales training; an age-old and aging business model that appeared to me to have stagnated.

Consider this: in 2004, when I wrote the **SELECT SELLING FIELDBOOK**, the sales training industry was nearly 35 years old. I have on my bookshelf a book called *Consultative Selling* (Hanan, Cribbin & Heiser), published in 1970 by the American Management Association. The opening sentence in the book might lift your spirits or cause you a wry smile:

> In the language of the salesman, there is a "whole new ball game" in selling today.

Roll the clock forward to 2004 and the sales training industry had changed little over that time. No dominant player had emerged. The market was highly fragmented, and in many sectors the dance between buyer and sales training provider was a revolving door of different suppliers claiming unique methodologies, or distinctive plays (forever leveraging sports analogies) to respond to the "whole new ball game."

However, what struck me most notably was the complete absence of meaningful software support for this important endeavor. And it is important and worthwhile: applying sales methodology effectively will dramatically impact your sales effectiveness. For decades studies have shown that effective use of sales methodology has a direct correlation with improved performance. But when assessing the landscape for supporting the application of sales methodology, the sales professional looked around her, and all she saw was a wasteland. Standing beside her counterparts from the Finance department with software that itself was well-rooted in accounting principles, or her colleagues from Marketing as they refined their customer profiling with automated A/B testing, or the Customer Service teams she depended on – who themselves depended on their automated knowledge system to support her customers – the sales professional, anxious, under pressure, and looking to improve herself, could reasonably wonder why she didn't have access to intelligent automated systems that 'knew' about sales methodology.

I recall speaking to a friend of mine who then was Senior Vice President of Sales for Expedia Corporate Travel (now Egencia). She and I had done business together before when I was running a previous software company. Her frustration at traditional sales training approaches was founded in many failed training initiatives. Recognizing the deficiencies of learning programs that were principally classroom- or eLearning-based, her challenge to me was simple: "Can't you just take all of your software knowledge, and figure out a way where the sales team will just learn what they need to learn when they need to learn it, and make it easy enough, and smart enough, so that they will continue to use it and learn-by-doing?"

Coming from a background of 20 years of building enterprise software applications, I wondered about what could happen if we re-imagined the delivery model for sales training. Surely there was a better way to learn than sitting in a classroom for a three-day training program, only to forget in a month the majority of what was taught? Surely sales methodology should be applied and available when the sales person was working their sales opportunity – and wasn't that most often when they were using their Customer Relationship Management (CRM) system.

Then I got excited as I considered the benefits of an integrated sales performance system, measuring progress, responding intelligently, and sustaining the learning through embedded context-sensitive advice. If the promise of sales methodology was to be realized, then intelligent software seemed to be the obvious route. I gathered together some of the team who had worked with me in my previous companies. Some of us had worked together in a company during the 1980s and 1990s where we built Artificial Intelligence systems. The possibilities for a sales system that got smarter with more use seemed a realistic goal. Imagine having a knowledgeable virtual sales coach available 24/7. What if we could eliminate the need for sales forecast calls through software that, based on experience, would 'know' when the opportunity would close? Or maybe it was possible to determine which opportunities you were more likely to win – guiding your allocation or prioritization of resources. The concept was thrilling.

We came up with a vision for how a sales organization might learn online, apply online, use online and coach online. We conceived a product called Dealmaker and were on our way. I had said to my friends that I would not do it again – but here I was with my fifth software start-up: Select Selling Inc.

But this was 2005, and there were not that many business application companies that had 'gone online.' The one clear exception was salesforce.com – in truth a band of zealots led by Marc Benioff, who were stargazing and prophesying a utopian vision of "No software" that has since proven to be less quixotic than their detractors predicted.

We looked at everything that salesforce.com did: we located our hosting infrastructure in the same building as salesforce.com; we studied their license agreements, and we borrowed from their pricing paradigm; we copied the Salesforce Foundation model as we too believed in 'doing good while doing well;' we learned from their marketing messaging; we analyzed their product management approach; we spoke to their customers and their employees; and we began our annual trek to Dreamforce. Then we decided to integrate Dealmaker with the salesforce.com CRM application.

In 2005 we released the first version of Dealmaker for salesforce.com. It was in fact the first sales methodology on the AppExchange – the marketplace for business applications integrated with Salesforce – and as our company was founded in Ireland, we were recognized as the first European application on the AppExchange.

Around that same time, Oracle acquired Siebel – and while that might seem like a *non sequitur*, the relevance will soon become apparent. In 1999 Siebel had acquired OnTarget, a leader in the sales methodology market, and owner and author of Target Account Selling (TAS) and other tremendous intellectual property around sales methodologies (including the Enterprise Selling Process and the Portfolio Management Process Account Planning method). As we entered the market in 2005 we came across many TAS fans – particularly those who were using it embedded in Siebel CRM. So after Oracle acquired Siebel, we purchased the OnTarget business unit from Oracle in July 2006 and changed our company name from Select Selling Inc. to The TAS Group.

Now we had a cloud-based enterprise class software application integrated with Dealmaker, the world's leading sales methodology, and a passion to drive change. We had unique value as the result of combining two disciplines: intelligent software applications, and deep sales methodologies. With innovation in our blood and at the core of our efforts, we began our journey in earnest to change the sales training industry fundamentally.

That was seven years ago, and, as you would expect, Dealmaker has changed a lot over that period. The 'smarts' have gotten smarter, and the methodologies have been significantly extended and updated to reflect the changing dynamics in the economy, the pervasiveness of the Internet, and the arrival of social networks and consequent evolving nature of buyer-seller interactions. In this book, I have tried to capture the essence of these experiences as they relate to Account Planning.

Over that time, salesforce.com has changed dramatically too. From its modest beginnings as a provider of Sales Force Automation (SFA) to small businesses, it has morphed into the leader in cloud computing, and is a real enterprise software provider covering sales, service, marketing, and more recently human capital management. It has become a viable online platform for software development and has charted the 'social' territory in enterprise organizations with its Chatter application. For two years running it has been cited as 'The Most Innovative Company in the World' by *Forbes* magazine – a truly remarkable accolade to receive when you consider the innovation from companies like Apple, Google and others during that same time.

Our partnership with salesforce.com also has evolved during that period and has become more strategic. We could be the poster-child for the Force.com platform as a development vehicle. It has been a tremendous experience for us. Dealmaker is now deployed as a native Force.com application. That means that Dealmaker is hosted in the Sales Cloud, running on the same servers, adhering to the same security model, and with complete integration between Dealmaker and the underlying CRM data. We couldn't be more 'joined-at-the-hip.'

Similarly salesforce.com has recognized the value that we provide with our Dealmaker software and sales methodologies. The wheel came full circle in 2012 when salesforce.com recognized our expertise in Account Planning and Management and signed a contract to become a Dealmaker user. This was a momentous event for our partnership.

Coupled with that we receive phenomenal support from salesforce.com in our go-to-market activity, and advice on our technical strategy and product direction. We are fortunate to get assistance in customer engagements, and the leadership at the world's leading cloud software company provides a constant compass as we plot our path to achieve optimal synergy between our two companies to the benefit of our joint customers.

In some ways this book, **ACCOUNT PLANNING *in* SALESFORCE**, is a celebration of the partnership between the two companies, but its core *raison d'être* is to improve the efficacy of salesforce.com's customers in Account Planning.

Account Planning is a tremendously important endeavor. It drives revenue, increases customer satisfaction, aligns your organization, and provides incredibly gratifying moments when you can see the impact of your work – both for the customer, and for your company.

We are constantly impressed by the wisdom of the experienced sales professionals, account planners and strategic account managers we have been privileged to work with, and are grateful for their tenacity and insights. I hope that this book has captured some of the value they shared with us and has amplified it somewhat through our continuing sales methodology research and innovation in sales performance automation.

We have tried to encapsulate the best of our experience and knowledge and improve it with the wisdom of salesforce.com and the sales community. Any shortcomings or mediocrities are mine alone.

Donal Daly
Cork, Ireland
January 2013

CHAPTER 1

WHY ACCOUNT PLANNING MATTERS

This is a book about maximizing revenue from large customers, about helping you to unlock revenue from big customers to turn them into bigger customers.

But perhaps I should pose a question right from the start:

> Do you need a different approach when you are selling to big companies just because they are big?

What's the matter with just using the very same methods that have worked in smaller companies? Are there really considerations that are so dramatically different that they call into question the basic techniques that succeed elsewhere?

The answer is both "Yes" and "No." Yes, you need a different approach, but no, you do not need to throw out techniques that succeed elsewhere. Instead I will build upon them, extending the basic concepts, and augmenting the methodology to yield a model more suitable to the size of the task at hand. The factor that drives the need for this reinforced 'industrial-strength' process can be captured in one word: *scale*.

The fact is that a large company is usually a collection of small, interrelated commercial activities, organized by function or geography, specialism or purpose, competitive forces or market dynamics. When approaching any such ecosystem, a deliberate design is demanded. Optimal outcomes are rarely achieved without such diligent efforts.

In early 2010, International Turnkey Systems (ITS), a 3,000-employee integrated information technology solutions and software services provider, deployed an integrated Account Planning and Opportunity Management system. The ITS Account Planning function spanned 45 countries and many virtual teams that each managed separate divisions of their largest customers.

Prior to the completion of the Account Planning project, communication and collaboration was difficult, and each division in each separate country was managed as a separate Account. With the introduction of the Account Management infrastructure, the Account Teams gained a single view of their customers, a deeper understanding of all of the business issues that their customers faced, and an enhanced ability to service each Account in a cohesive manner. By the middle of 2011, the investment paid off, and the return on the initiative was impressive. ITS measured a number of Key Performance Indicators and recorded these results:

- The number of opportunities increased by 47% through better awareness of the customer's Business Initiatives, resulting in an ability to 'create' new sales opportunities.
- With a deeper understanding of the benefit that could be gained by the customer, ITS could focus more on the value that could be delivered. Deals grew in size, and became less sensitive to price. Average deal size was up 26%.
- Citing closer relationships and more non-competitive deals, ITS achieved a 58% improvement in win rate by winning opportunities of which the competitors were not even aware.

- Because ITS understood the impact of each of the customer's Business Initiatives, and the extent of the problems that had to be addressed, it was able to maintain momentum in the sales cycle and reduced the average sales cycle length by 27%.
- Measured together, these factors contributed to a 400% increase in overall sales velocity for ITS!

Also, when ITS started the project, only 37% of management were using Salesforce, and a little over 50% of the sales team were putting in their opportunities. Having implemented this new Account Planning discipline, using Dealmaker Smart Account Manager integrated with Salesforce, 90% of managers were now using the system to manage their business.

In **CHAPTER 2: THE CUSTOMER FIRST,** I will discuss the benefits of putting the customer at the center of all of your Account Planning efforts, and explore the journey that customers usually take from *Prospect*, to *Customer*, to *Loyal Customer*, and then, seemingly inevitably, to *Former Customer*. Account Planning can help accelerate the first part of this journey and help you put the brakes on before customers take that exit ramp. Customer retention is one of the key benefits of Account Planning and Management, but there are many others.

Account Planning is a strategic imperative that goes beyond traditional selling tactics. The benefits that accrue go beyond simple revenue numbers, and point to an approach that must be focused not just on greater revenue as the sole arbiter of strategy. When Account Planning is executed well, customer satisfaction increases. Customers who are more satisfied buy more from you, and do so without calling your competitors first. Customers who are served well are easier to retain, and therefore it is easier to make your revenue targets year after year. When you do effective Account Planning, you get to understand the customer's business, sit with them at their side of the table, and strengthen your ability to shape their thinking and their business strategies. A happy customer is hostile territory for your competitor to enter. Switching suppliers is expensive for a customer and they will do so only if they feel you are not serving them well and fairly. Your ability to monitor, measure and react is greater if you are closer to the heart of their business, understanding their corporate goals, and motivations. It takes investment, research and hard work, but is the price of customer retention and growth.

> When Xerox spent $6.4bn in 2010 to purchase Affiliated Computer Services (ACS), the goal was to accelerate Xerox's transformation into a global services company providing world-class business process management and outsourcing services.
>
> For Ursula Burns, the new CEO at Xerox, this was potentially a defining moment, early in her CEO tenure. In a statement announcing the deal she said, "By combining Xerox's strengths in document technology with ACS's expertise in managing and automating work processes, we're creating a new class of solution provider." The statement went on to say, "Xerox is confident it will achieve significant incremental revenue growth by leveraging Xerox's strong global brand and established client relationships to scale ACS's business in Europe, Asia and South America. In addition, Xerox will integrate its intellectual property with ACS's services to create new solutions for end-to-end support of customers' work processes."
>
> According to Pat Elizondo, a Senior Vice President at Xerox, speaking during a session on Strategic Account

Management at salesforce.com's Dreamforce event late in 2011, the acquisition brought with it both challenges and opportunities. Elizondo was charged with supporting the integration of the two companies.

The challenges were the obvious ones. Of course there were different cultures, different management processes, various approaches to Account Planning, and multiple sales reps calling on the same Account. On the other hand however, the opportunities were immense, and of course reflected the ambition articulated by the Xerox CEO. There were many complementary capabilities and assets from the two companies, which would lead to great cross-sell opportunities, and increased openings to sell a broader portfolio of solutions to a larger customer base. The core question was how to unlock that treasure trove in a managed way without slowing down either business. It was a bit like changing the tires on a car while speeding down the highway.

Account Planning was critical to the integration, and it turned out to be very effective. The results that Elizondo presented at Dreamforce, less than two years after the acquisition, were impressive:

- 400% increase in pipeline where joint Account Planning was executed.
- $5bn in potential contracts generated in New Business Synergy pipeline.
- Increase in trust and collaboration across the joint Account Teams.

The benefits of Account Planning are available to all companies, not just those going through a major upheaval. If you have even one Large Account then Account Planning is worth the effort. Maximizing revenue from your existing customers is the single most effective way to grow revenue. If you manage a group of named Accounts, then the same principles apply – I refer to that as 'Portfolio Planning.' Each individual Account may represent a division in your notional Large Account – your territory.

As markets and economies have become increasingly volatile, the costs and risks associated with a business model predicated on continuous new customer acquisition are trending skywards. Most successful companies, and the sales professionals who lead the way to their annual President's Club trips, are being more selective in the customers they pursue, and are doing more business with those that they win. They recognize that losing a customer is not just a loss for them but also a win for their competitor, thereby making that competitor stronger and more formidable in the future.

As 2013 unfolds, my prediction is that Account Planning will eclipse general marketing as a source of opportunities for revenue growth among winning sales professionals. The ubiquity of the Internet, your customer's ability to find out about your products and services as quickly as you can yourself, the impact on social networks as a driver of influence and preference, the pervasiveness of mobile devices providing always-on communication, and the growing barriers to customer acquisition all mean that you can no longer be a generalist in your market. You need to be a specialist and expert in the business, strategy and market of those few customers with whom you are working.

Account Planning methodology today – as described in this book – is an evolution of the sales skills you have used in the past. It must be built on a solid foundation. Many of the fundamental tenets that form the cornerstone of that foundation are referenced in the early chapters of this book. But as you reach for greater account penetration, longer lasting relationships, higher levels of customer satisfaction, and a true partnership with your customers, a different approach is required. It will be an augmentation of solid opportunity management – but on a broader scale, combining research, marketing, business strategy, competitive analysis, and very targeted positioning to leverage your unique sustainable differential advantage as you seek to uncover opportunities that can deliver Mutual Value – value to you in tandem with value to your customer. As you participate in the race for greater revenue attainment, Account Planning is more a marathon than a sprint, but yet gets you over the line faster.

David is a strong sales performer. He knows his industry very well. In the five years prior to the start of this story, he worked in a field sales role, and had achieved or come close to quota every year. The majority of David's customers are medium size businesses, in the $1bn to $5bn range, and he was established as a Trusted Advisor to the buyers in those organizations.

While David was out there making his numbers, his company was going through some changes. The company's offerings and the market in which it operated had begun to mature. The executive leadership made a strategic decision to place a greater focus on larger accounts, in addition to the medium size businesses where David had been very successful. David was recognized as a top performer and a consistent contributor. He was asked to lead a team to focus on a large-scale enterprise account that I will call Megacorp Inc. David was excited, but was sufficiently seasoned to know that he should temper his enthusiasm until he had done some investigation.

When David logged on to Salesforce CRM and looked up Megacorp, he was pleased to see that the marketing team had done preliminary research and entered data about Megacorp into the system. He was a little surprised to see that there were 47 different Account Records created for

> Megacorp. After some quick online research David uncovered that Megacorp had $50bn revenue, 90,000 employees, seven major business divisions, major operations in 42 countries, 17 acquisitions in the past five years, and a rapidly changing competitive landscape. This was a much bigger and much more complex Account than David had ever encountered before. He did not really know where to start.
>
> But, one of David's greatest strengths was that he was never afraid to ask for help, and that was where we got to hear his story and help him grow Megacorp into one of his company's largest customers.

David's situation at Megacorp is not uncommon. When faced with the challenge of developing or growing a Large Account, or any Account with multiple discrete buying units, the very scale of the opportunity can be daunting. In fact we learned that David could have done more in his medium size customers when he admitted to us that he was very opportunity-focused – and not at all account-focused. When I speak with experienced sales professionals, they all admit to having had a similar situation at some point in their own sales career. If fact, it seems almost a certainty that, as sales practitioners evolve from novice to maturity, each and every one suffers from a comparable experience. To some extent, we are all cut from the same cloth, and perhaps, if you examine your own activities today, I wonder whether you can find some of David's early behavior. There's good and bad in that realization. The *bad* is that you have undoubtedly made less money than you may have done; the *good* is that you have yet a treasure trove to uncover.

When looking at the customer from an Account perspective, there is a fundamental shift in thinking required before any sale can be made, and that is where Account Planning and Account Management comes in.

You will notice that, in the cases of both ITS and Xerox, they approached their customers more in a strategic marketing sense rather than as a set of disconnected opportunities. Their Account Planning initiatives required a different perspective – let's explore that now.

The Account as a Marketplace

When thinking about Account Planning I like to think of my Account as a marketplace that I want to lead. If there are enough discrete target areas in the Account, then I must take that approach. Thinking of it this way gives me reason to pause and think strategically about where in the marketplace I should focus. Are there market segments that are more attractive than others? Are there some that I should avoid? How do I know?

Looking at my Account as a marketplace naturally will encourage me to apply proven go-to-market principles. It encourages me to consider the market landscape, the total addressable market – the amount being spent by the customer with all suppliers in all areas that are applicable to all of my solutions – and to analyze the competitive landscape, uncovering incumbent players and emerging entrants.

Figure 1: The Marketplace

Based on the market requirements – which are really the customer's Business Needs – I can prioritize and focus my efforts and I can reflect on where my short-term and long-term focus should be. A structured Account Planning approach challenges me to reflect on what go-to-market partners I should consider, and how I might market to the Account, creating initial awareness that I can subsequently translate to interest in, and preference for, my company and its solutions.

By taking this approach, Account Planning can help you to maximize the return you get from a key existing Account or new strategic Account. An Account Planning methodology can be your compass as you navigate your marketplace.

As in David's situation in the Megacorp case, Account Planning is usually a team sport, one where you engage other people in your company to help in both the planning and the execution of your Account Strategy. The mission of the Account Team is to:

> Build long-term business relationships in a complex marketplace that enable you to create, develop, pursue, and win business that delivers mutual value.

I think this is important enough to spell out:

- Build *long-term* business relationships ...
- In a complex *marketplace* ...
- That enable you to *create, develop, pursue, and win business* ...
- That delivers *mutual value.*

In order to create the long-term relationships that you need, you must be able to understand the complex marketplace that is the customer. Understanding the customer allows you to identify and create value for them, because you understand their needs and know how to address them. In turn, you create value for your company because you can identify, develop, and pursue new opportunities in the Account long before your competition has any inkling of those opportunities.

The Missed Opportunity

Since 2007 The TAS Group has been conducting research into the state of the global sales effectiveness industry. The latest incarnation of this research is the 2012 Dealmaker Index Global Benchmark Study. Based on an analysis of 92 sales performance factors, mapped against proven successful approaches, the Dealmaker Index measures the effectiveness of sales organizations and sales individuals across areas such as deal close rates, sales cycle management, account management, value creation and sales opportunity development.

When we analyzed the results around Account Planning, it transpired that just over half (53%) of sales professionals are effective at maximizing revenue from key Accounts. If you feel that you are not optimally effective at this important sales task, you can take some comfort in the fact that you are not alone.

Figure 2: The Missed Opportunity

53%
of sales reps are effective at
maximizing revenue from key accounts
Revenue
Impact
And those reps are
41% more likely to achieve quota
Source: Dealmaker Index

But look at the size of the opportunity that is being missed. Unsurprisingly, when you get your key accounts humming – you are much more likely to make quota.

We asked sales leaders to measure the effectiveness of their sales organizations at scaling their business in their largest customers. For those same organizations we measured the percentage of the sales team who achieved quota. Sales professionals who are effective at maximizing revenue from their key accounts are 41% more likely to make quota.

Sales people don't necessarily always like to plan. Many take a view that when they are planning, they are not selling. Yes, it is true. How about you? What do you think? Answer these questions honestly:

- As a professional sales person, do you enjoy the annual task of planning?
- Do you like the annual request from your sales leadership to build out how you are going to be successful achieving your quota for next year?

I can hear the groaning from here.

But acquiring new customers is 500% more expensive than retaining existing ones – and the 41% quota improvement is pretty compelling. It really *is* worth the effort.

The Three Core Themes

There are a number of components to the Account Planning and Management methodology described in this book. I will shortly focus on the three core themes, but first I will describe the journey we will travel together.

You will learn how to gather the information you need to understand the Account as a marketplace and to segment that marketplace into discrete units so that you can choose where to spend your time. Recording the Current Opportunities in the Account, as well as business you already have won, you will be able to place your solutions on a structured map of the customer's business.

Exploring how to uncover the customer's Business Drivers and how to navigate the political landscape in the account will help you to understand both the people who matter – the Key Players – and their associated Business Drivers.

When all of the opportunities in the Account have been identified, you will evaluate each one against the twin axes of *Value to Customer* and *Value to Us*. That way you will uncover areas of *Mutual Value* – which is a thread that you will find woven into the fabric of the methodology. It is important. This is the *White Space* in the Account where you can help your customer to identify new potential areas of opportunity – and simultaneously discover new areas of opportunity for yourself.

Finally, I will demonstrate how you build the Execution Plan so that you get beyond planning and begin to manage and execute.

And to keep things interesting, you will find many musical references throughout the book. I guarantee you that this will be the only book on Account Planning that you will find that includes a song playlist. Who said Account Planning couldn't be enjoyable?

There are three core themes that I would like to introduce now – and reprise later – that are fundamental to maximizing the revenue that you can achieve from your Large Accounts:

1. Research for Insight.
2. Integrate for Velocity.
3. Focus for Impact.

Research for Insight

There is frequently a contradiction between the importance that sales leaders profess they place on Account Planning and their actual behavior. While recognizing the tremendous value that can accrue from this important sales discipline, they habitually revert to type and look for the deal that they can close quickly.

When Larry Williams, an American rhythm and blues singer, released his *Dizzy Miss Lizzie* single in 1958, the B-side of the single was a song called *Slow Down*. Subsequently covered by The Beatles, The Jam, Led Zeppelin, The Flamin' Groovies, Brian May of Queen, and included on a joint Jools

Holland / Tom Jones album in 2005, the title and lyrics are a good reminder of a basic principle of Account Planning, as it relates to the pursuits of individual opportunities:

Slow down, baby,
Baby, now you're movin' way too fas'

Slow Down, Larry Williams, 1958

In the real estate and retail industries, the cliché goes "It's all about location, location, and location." If you are hoping to maximize revenue from your large accounts, it is really all about research, research, and research. You need to slow down your natural inclination to pursue deals now. If you do your homework on the account, and apply the experience you have gained from working with other customers, you should be able to bring insight to the customer. If you don't do the research, then you won't have the knowledge, and then you can't bring insight – and that is a missed opportunity.

Later, in **CHAPTER 4: RESEARCH FOR INSIGHT**, I will outline the knowledge you need to uncover to inform the basis of your insight. Gaining insight is not always easy. It is something special, something that not everyone knows and so you have to work to find it. Insight is derived from knowledge, information and experience, and is a currency that, once earned, should be spent wisely.

Remember, your role is to create value for the customer, not just to communicate information about your company or your solutions. Before you position your value, a prerequisite is having a deep sense of what the customer values. When you have done your research, you can begin to feel comfortable in the customer's shoes, and begin the walk together toward Mutual Value.

Integrate for Velocity

A few years back I did some consulting work for a Fortune 20 company. I was shocked to learn about their process for building their go-to-market plans.

Every sales person who had responsibility for a Large Account was given a 60-slide PowerPoint template that they were asked to fill out. There were 1,500 Large Accounts that had to be covered. Then all of the 1,500 PowerPoint decks were emailed to a sales operations person who typed all of the data from the decks into a single enormous Excel spreadsheet. The sales operations person aggregated and analyzed all of the input from the 1,500 plans – yes, 1,500 PowerPoint decks! – and then submitted the result to executive management for review. The time lapse between the completion of the PowerPoint plans and the submission for executive review was three months. Only then could the sales person discuss their plan with their customer, or begin to execute on the plan.

The obvious problems with this approach included:

- The Account Plans were developed without any reference to the overall market. Little thought was given to the macro market factors that were common across the plans. That resulted in the recommended actions in one plan being in direct conflict with the direction of another plan in a similar market segment.
- There was no opportunity for collaboration with the customer to gain agreement that the Account Plan would address their Business Drivers.
- Much of the data that was used in the development of the plan was recorded already in the company's CRM system, but of course there was no integration between the CRM system and the PowerPoint-based Account

Plans. During the three-month time lapse between Account Plan development and executive review, the data in the CRM changed – so the plans were out-of-date before they were even reviewed.

- Since the plans were PowerPoint-based, it was incredibly difficult for the Account Team to brainstorm ideas together, share the plan, or contribute individual thoughts to the account strategy.

Unsurprisingly, this Account Planning initiative failed. Account Planning should be considered in the context of an integrated sales ecosystem as part of your go-to-market activity.

Figure 3: An Integrated Sales Ecosystem

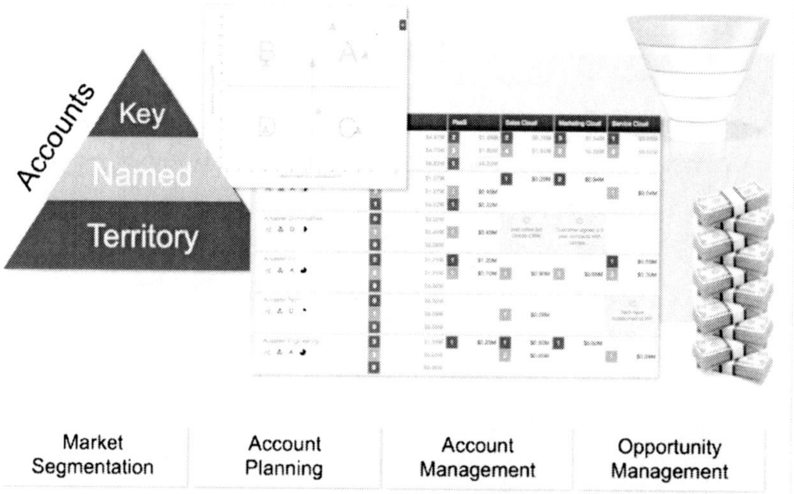

Account Planning should not be an annual event. It is not about reporting what you know; it is about discovering what you don't know, and then acting to uncover the missing information to inform your subsequent activity.

Account Planning must live and breathe as part of how you run your business. It needs to become part of your culture, and should be integrated into your overall business cadence.

A single Account is a subset of your overall market, and a composite representation of all of the individual real and potential prospective opportunities within that Account. You must recognize it as an integrated component of the market ecosystem.

When you are developing an Account Plan, it would be foolhardy to do so without considering the whole story, and all of the players who can contribute. You need to make it easy to adopt Account Planning and management as part of your company's processes.

I will explore this in more detail in **CHAPTER 5: INTEGRATE FOR VELOCITY**, but in simple terms, you need to integrate data, knowledge and information to achieve velocity. The data already exists in Salesforce, your Account Team has the knowledge, and the customer has the information. The whole is much greater than the sum of the parts when they work seamlessly together.

Later, in **CHAPTER 4: RESEARCH FOR INSIGHT**, I will examine this more closely, and you can explore how Dealmaker Smart Account Manager combined with Salesforce can help you achieve your velocity goals. I am not sure I know how you can achieve the required level of organizational velocity without some form of smart Account Planning software system integrated with Salesforce.

Focus for Impact

This book is called **ACCOUNT PLANNING *in* SALESFORCE**. It is focused on helping companies that have purchased Salesforce with their Account Planning initiatives. It does not pretend to be as helpful to customers who use other CRM systems. Whether I believe that the principles outlined here have generic relevance or not is in itself irrelevant. Focusing on Salesforce enables me to provide Mutual Value and deliver a greater impact to this specific community because I can have a deeper understanding of the elements that are most critical to Salesforce users. My goal is for this book to be the reference text on Account Planning for all Salesforce users. I believe this degree of focus is hugely powerful, and I know that it has helped me tremendously in this project.

Focus is the parallel thread that runs alongside Mutual Value from the beginning to the end of this book. It is in fact the catalyst for Mutual Value, driving you to uncover areas that benefit you and the customer. Later in **CHAPTER 6: SEGMENT FOR PRIORITY** you will see how you can select which divisions or Business Units in an account are in your 'sweet spot,' that area where you can uniquely and competitively deliver true value. Then in **CHAPTER 9: FOCUS FOR IMPACT**, you will see again how to make some hard choices as you target the opportunities on which to focus – those that deliver Mutual Value – while at the same time choosing not to apply resources to less attractive opportunities.

According to the Dealmaker Index study, sales professionals who qualify well are 58% more likely to make quota. Focus is the ultimate form of sales qualification, deciding what you should pursue, and what is better left to the side. You are qualifying the market, each business segment in the account and, of course, each sales opportunity. That is how you deliver most impact.

Before You Continue ...

Planning is never the most fun thing any of us do. It requires discipline and stamina, and provides very little immediate gratification. But you need to keep your eye on the prize. On average you will see a 41% improvement in revenue achievement. But then, you are not average, are you? You can probably do better.

On the other hand, you might choose not to plan at all and enjoy blissful ignorance, never knowing the opportunity you've missed. Here's a thought:

> The nice thing about not planning is that failure comes as a complete surprise and is not preceded by a period of worry and depression. (John Preston, Boston College)

If you use the right tools, and follow the map I've laid out in this book, you will build great Account Plans and do so much more easily than you ever dreamed possible. Not only that, but you will deliver more value to your customers, and build long-term relationships that will serve you well through your career.

Of course, there is always the increase in revenue that will accrue from your efforts when you reach that destination with your customer.

Thanks for joining me on the journey.

CHAPTER 2

THE CUSTOMER FIRST

The primary purpose of **ACCOUNT PLANNING *in* SALESFORCE** is to outline a framework that you might choose to use to inform your Account Planning approach. As described in the subtitle, the goal of the book is to help you to *Unlock Revenue in Big Customers to Turn Them into BIGGER Customers.* However, before we get into the mechanics of Account Planning, it is important to understand the customers' frame of reference, the mindset they are bringing to the conversation, and the perspective that informs their behavior.

In this chapter, and also in **CHAPTER 3: THE TRUST DEFAULT** and **CHAPTER 5: INTEGRATE FOR VELOCITY**, I take a peek inside the minds of the business buyers and give my observations on how things are influenced by the changing nature of their business environment.

You may find some of these observations obvious, but there may be a few that might give you reasons to pause, perhaps taking a broader perspective than you might otherwise have done. If that happens once or twice, then your Account Planning activity will be more productive and it may be sufficient return for the investment you have made in reading this book.

Everything starts with your customers, of course. Your relationship changes with them through the many interactions that you have. If you are successful, you will develop a connection or bond, an appropriate alliance that serves both parties well. But first you must appreciate that the voyage you are on together has many crossroads, on- and off-ramps, junctions and stops. It starts before they become a customer, and usually ends, unfortunately, when they become a former customer. There are many pivotal points along the way, but there are few more intense than when you are approaching a buying decision moment.

In this chapter I take a broad look at the journey from Prospect to Former Customer, and include some thoughts on the changing disposition of the buyer as she approaches the buying decision moment.

Remember this:

> The impact on a customer of a poor buying decision is usually greater than the impact on a sales person of a lost deal.

It may be a useful perspective to retain in all of the interactions with your customer. It makes you think about the impact on the customer – and that is a good thing.

The Four Phases of Customer Evolution

There are only four customer phases, and all customers will be in one of these at all times. There are many erudite articles written about the interdependence between sales processes and buying processes, but – being primarily focused on new customer acquisition – many miss a critical consideration: the Four Phases of Customer Evolution: from Prospect, to Customer, to Loyal Customer and, finally, to Former Customer.

Figure 4: The Four Phases of Customer Evolution

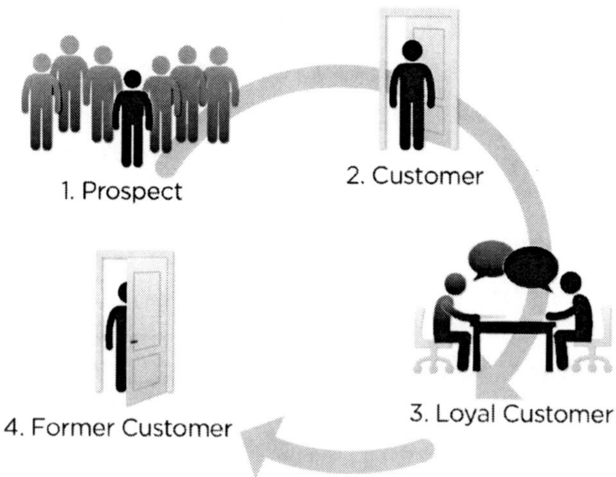

Customers go through three Growing Phases and one Dying Phase. You should understand the phases and, in particular, the reason why customers move from the Growth Phases to the Dying Phase. The critical thing is not just to recognize which phase they are in – that is fairly obvious – but to understand that, if they are to become a customer, then they will inevitably morph from phase to phase. It is only a matter of time.

The fundamental substance of all the management theory, strategic advice and best practice writings about Customer Management, Key Account Management or Account Planning might be summarized as follows:

> Accelerate the transition through the three Growing Phases, from Prospect to Customer to Loyal Customer and decelerate the inevitable transition to Former Customer in the Dying Phase.

Acquiring and Retaining Customers

Think about how you make a big purchase. Perhaps it is something really major like a house or a car, or maybe something less dramatic like a replacement set of golf clubs. As you begin researching your purchase, your emotions are deeply engaged and, while you're generally interested in making sure that whatever you are buying is within your price range, you're focused on your needs. Is the house in the right location and big enough to do all the entertaining you're planning? Can the technology in the new golf clubs compensate for a certain lack of technique, and you always needed a two-seater sports car anyway – right? You view the house, test-drive the car, or swing the club, and now you're a little more focused on the details. You're visiting schools, shops and other amenities in the area, making sure the house isn't overrun by termites, and investigating the structural integrity of that extra room that was added last year. You're reading the J.D. Power survey, checking the automobile insurance costs and considering the residual value of the car, all the while testing out the response to "Me? I drive a Porsche" in the singles bars, and wondering "Rory McIlroy can drive the ball 300 yards with this club, is there any reason why I can't?"

Now, it's the time to make up your mind and sign up. "What, are you crazy? Sign up to pay a prince's ransom every month for 30 years, just for a place to sleep? You must think I'm mad! Why would I pay the price of a small house for a car that only has two seats? Maybe I should get a few golf lessons before I spend that amount of money on a set of clubs? I'm really not that keen on the game anyway."

The buying process is a funny thing. People often use information and data after the fact to rationalize the very personal emotional decisions made during the buying process. While this behavior may be more often true in personal consumer purchases than in the corporate buying process, it is important to understand the different legs of the journey that your customers will travel as they move towards their buying decision. The emotional influences are still at play, even if they have been formulized or regularized through the corporation's procurement process.

All through the professional buying cycle, buyers are concerned about risk and the price of your offering. They seek evidence that you are the best supplier, and need to be assured that you can meet their needs. However, the buyer's primary emphasis changes throughout the buying cycle and they focus on different concerns at different times. It is important to know where you are in the cycle and to understand what's occupying the buyer's mind at that time.

To join the buyer on her travels, I have segmented the buying cycle into just four main stages. I use the terms Requirements, Evidence, Acquisition and Post-Sale. Not all buying-cycle analysis includes Post-Sale, and I think that is a mistake, particularly in relation to Account Planning and Management. In this context – and perhaps this should be a golden rule in all selling – a sales person's key asset is his customer. He needs to be involved after the deal has been consummated, to maintain the relationship, to continue to serve the customer, and to seek out other opportunities.

In **Figure 5** below I highlight the relative importance of each concern throughout the process.

Figure 5: The Buying Cycle

	Requirements	Evidence	Acquisition	Post-Sale
Needs	**Critical**	High	Low	Medium
Risk	Low	Medium	**Critical**	High
Solution	Low	**Critical**	Medium	Medium
Price	Medium	Low	**Critical**	Low

Early in the procurement cycle, the buyer will check briefly on price to make sure your offering is in the general area of her expected budget. At this point, it's all about her needs, her wants and her process. Getting past the first checkpoint requires that you pass the basic features test. Can your offering meet the needs of the customer? If not, the price doesn't matter.

So far the customer has little risk, as no major irrevocable decisions are being made. This is the Requirements stage of the buying cycle. Your opportunity to shape the customer's requirements is strongest in this phase of the buying cycle.

Leaving the Requirements stage behind and entering the Evidence stage, the customer now requires very specific data from you to substantiate your claims that you can meet the needs that she outlined. You must prove to her, or more likely the buying committee, that you understand her requirements and that your solution is all it's cracked up to be. As she invests more time, her risk is increasing but her focus remains pinpointed on your evidence. This will probably include detailed examination of your offering, reference calls to other customers, future support, product vision and more specific price discussions. Likely as not, the customer will reduce her list of potential suppliers at this time.

It's still like buying a car or a house. You're down to a choice of two or three, all of which meet your needs, each with sufficient evidence to assuage your concerns about whether you're getting everything you expect – but now you're getting a little nervous.

As the customer is making the final choice and is getting ready to sign on the dotted line, she is reaching the buying decision moment, and the sale is possibly at its most vulnerable. She is now more nervous than at any other time in the cycle. Up to now, there is always a way out – but once the decision is made, it's done, over, complete. Better not screw up now.

This is where the professional sales person understands the need for positive reinforcement and a restatement for the buyer of the rationale for the buying decision. If you have done your job well up to now, you and the buyer will have arrived at this conclusion together.

In this, the Acquisition stage, all the work done up to now can be for naught if the buyer gets butterflies and isn't comfortable to proceed. Risk is uppermost in her mind, and price rears its head again. "So if I'm going do this, you need to give me a deal." Sometimes the buyer needs something extra, or a price concession, to make her feel good about making the decision and to help her over the line. This is particularly true when one person will carry the responsibility for making the decision.

Risk fades as a factor in the buyer's mind after the purchase is made, but only to be replaced by anxiety. As they say, the proof of the pudding is in the eating, and until the new product or service has been fully implemented and bedded in, the buyer will still feel vulnerable. You must address that concern if you want to maintain a long-term relationship. Post-Sale, the buyer no longer cares about price. Real evidence is needed to prove to her that she made the right decision. Work hard at it, and reward her trust.

You just converted a Prospect to a Customer, and you will want to remain engaged, making sure that both you and your company deliver on your promises, if you want to help the customer make the transition to Loyal Customer.

Here are some specific actions you might take:

- Follow up with the customer to make certain her needs are being met and progress is as per expectation.
- Co-ordinate resources within your organization to resolve issues quickly.
- Maintain frequent communication with the customer to show your continued interest in his success.
- Be honest about problems and engage, not in blame allocation, but in problem resolution.
- Continue to develop your relationship with the customer for future mutual gain.
- After the sale, when all is going well, ask for a referral. Then continue to do your research to deliver further insights and to keep your seat at the executive table.

Also, one of the attributes of sales people most valued by executives is their continued marshaling of resources to support their needs. You will need to demonstrate your continued commitment to doing that on the customer's behalf to maintain their trust and their long-term business.

The Dying Phase

I don't need to tell you that acquiring new customers can be hard work. Look at the arduous journey you had to take to convert a Prospect to a Customer. You know it is much better to retain a customer, and to mine that asset for new business, than it is to start that cycle all over again. You want to convert that Customer to a Loyal Customer, and to avoid the seemingly inevitable transition to a Former Customer.

Let's consider why you really should care about this. Here are some facts to ponder:

- The cost of new customer acquisition is 500% that of customer retention.
- Increasing customer retention by 2% equates to decreasing costs by 10%.
- Reducing customer defections by 5% can increase profitability by up to 125% (depending on industry). (Source: *Leading on the Edge of Chaos*, Emmet C. Murphy and Mark A. Murphy)

I want you to consider the two different scenarios I have outlined below. Each is reflective of a real situation, and I hope you will easily identify with them both.

Scenario A

In the first scenario you (or your company) are selling a product or service to your customer. Think about a company that you used to have as a customer – but they have become a Former Customer. Stop and think for a minute about why they stopped doing business with you:

- Why have they left you or your company?
- What do you think are the top three reasons?

- Write them down – now, before you play out the next scenario.

1. ____________________________________
2. ____________________________________
3. ____________________________________

Scenario B

In the second scenario, you are the customer. You might be forgiven for thinking that being a customer is easier than being a supplier – but that is not always the case.

In this scenario, think about the last time you (or your company) decided to stop doing business with a particular source. If you take a personal perspective on this, that source might be a restaurant, a clothing store, a hairdresser, an online bookstore, an airline, or an online community. From the perspective of your company, the source may be your stationery provider, IT services supplier, sales trainer, telecommunication equipment vendor, or any one of many other options. Combine the personal and company perspectives (if you have both) and write down the top three reasons why you defected:

1. ____________________________________
2. ____________________________________
3. ____________________________________

If you are like most people, your answer to Scenario A will start with price or product features, and your answer to Scenario B is more likely to be more focused on 'how I was treated.' The problem is that, in the real world, the answers from these two scenarios converge and the disconnect between what suppliers think and the opinions of their customers sends their relationship hurtling from a Growing Phase straight into the spiral of the Dying Phase.

Why do customers leave? The reality might be different than you think. According to RightNow Technologies (now part of Oracle):

- 73% of customers leave because they are dissatisfied with customer service, but companies think just 21% leave for this reason.
- Companies think that nearly half (48%) of their customers leave because of price, when in fact, according to the customer perspective, this happens only 25% of the time.

The U.S. Small Business Administration and the U.S. Chamber of Commerce support these findings. Their research shows:

- 68% of customers leave because they are upset with the treatment they've received.
- Only 14% are dissatisfied with the product or service.

Serenade Your Customer

You've abandoned me.
Love don't live here anymore.

Love Don't Live Here Anymore, Rose Royce III: Strikes Again!, Royce Rose, 1978

The lyrics here are from the 1978 song *Love Don't Live Here Anymore* by Rose Royce, an American soul and R&B group that had a number of hit singles in the 1970s. While the reference to this song might be a little contrived – I'm a sucker for musical references – the sentiment is well expressed and relevant.

If your customers leave you, it is because they don't love you, and that is usually because they feel unloved. The reason they don't love you is usually because they feel you have abandoned them. If there is a vacuum, your competitor will rush to fill it – and your customer will become a former customer.

It is hard to accept that the reason your customers don't love you is because you have underserved them. It is much easier if you can point to price or product features as the determinants of defection. That hurts less because you can convince yourself that there is little you could have done about it.

Ask yourself this: if you knew that your customer was going to move from a Growing Phase to the Dying Phase, and there was nothing that you could do about price or product features, what actions would you take to serve them better so they would stay?

So what are you waiting for? Write down your answers – and take action now.

CHAPTER 3

THE TRUST DEFAULT

If you want to build a long-term customer relationship you need to develop a deep level of trust with that customer. Customer acquisition is easier when you are starting from a foundation of trust. Once you have a Customer, converting that Customer to a Loyal Customer will happen only if the Customer feels that she can depend on you. Unless you achieve that level of trust your Customer will become a Former Customer.

Trust is the fulcrum upon which every customer relationship pivots. Trust is a valuable currency that must be earned, but never spent. Trust is built one step at a time, and unless protected, can be blown away in a moment. Account Planning is all about developing long-term relationships, and that is hard to do without trust.

Here's an illuminating story.

> When Angela called one spring day, the excitement coming over Skype was contagious. Angela was CEO of Kincometrics, a small software company serving the pharmaceutical market. Recognizing that selling to large pharma companies was going to be very difficult for a small company, as part of her go-to-market strategy, Kincometrics had partnered with a large well-known enterprise software company. For the purpose of this story

– and to protect Angela's business – I will refer to that company as BigSoft.

Angela's face lit up as she told me that she had accompanied one of BigSoft's sales executives to a meeting with BigPharma. (No, that's not its name either!) The meeting had gone exceptionally well, and Kincometrics was on the verge of its largest deal ever.

In Angela's words, the background went something like this:

> *"BigPharma had put out a RFI to a number of regulatory compliance system (RCS) vendors. It's important to note that BigSoft does not have an RCS offering, so it would not have been able to complete the RFI without our company. They requested only three of the vendors to complete the RFP, and happily we were one of those. The RFP was followed up by web demos initially and then an on-site demo. The relationship between us, the BigSoft team and the BigPharma team started off really well.*
>
> *BigPharma's team felt more and more comfortable with the subject matter expertise of our team. The reason for this was that two thought leaders in our space represented Kincometrics. We had two PhDs (chemistry and microbiology) with extensive laboratory experience. As a result we could relate well to the day-to-day operations of the proposed end-users.*
>
> *A number of web meetings followed the visit and then another on-site demo and discussion about implementation. We highlighted the extremely tight partnership between Kincometrics and BigSoft. This was clearly important to James, the CIO from BigPharma. Pretty soon it became apparent to everyone on the team that James was leading the decision-making process here. He felt the need to have a vendor who not only had the correct technology solution but*

also had a clear focus on the pharmaceutical industry. This would provide them with the support to expand the implementation as BigPharma deployment grew."

Angela had called me to tell me that the meeting she had just attended was the final step in the budget approval process. She had won the business! Kincometrics was the preferred vendor and the price was acceptable. James, BigPharma's CIO, confirmed that he was very comfortable with Angela's team. He expressed his admiration for the unique design of Kincometrics's RCS software, and said he was reassured by the partnership with BigSoft. What could go wrong?

Unfortunately, the story did not end there. The next call I got from Angela was not as positive:

> "James requested a meeting with the new CEO of BigSoft, Kincometrics' partner, and made it clear that this meeting was just to confirm his decision that he could rely on the technology support and domain expertise of the joint team. He made it clear that he preferred the Kincometrics solution. His only concerns were ongoing support and confidence that BigSoft was sufficiently focused on BigPharma's future needs. Kincometrics was not represented at that meeting. That was a huge mistake.
>
> After the meeting between the CEO of BigSoft and BigPharma CIO, the BigSoft sales guy who was at the meeting said, "This was the worst meeting I've ever been at in 30 years of selling. Even though I prepared everything that the CEO needed to bring this deal home, he totally screwed it up." He was talking about his own CEO, the face of BigSoft!
>
> The BigSoft CEO spoke only of the many changes that he planned to make now that he had taken over at BigSoft. He talked about the other industries that he had yet to conquer: Government, Finance, etc. He

> talked ... and talked ... and talked, and did not listen to James, the BigPharma CIO. Two weeks later we got the news that BigPharma would stay with its incumbent system, making further modifications to that rather than deploying the Kincometrics package. It's a disaster!
>
> The CIO from BigPharma emailed me to say he was sorry, but he felt that he could not trust BigSoft because, even though he said otherwise, James felt that the CEO of BigSoft was following only his own agenda. The CEO promised him that he would support their deployment, but did not listen to BigPharma's concerns. The trust that Kincometrics had built up over the previous number of months was lost.
>
> To add to the irony of the situation, during the main-stage presentation at the BigSoft Sales Kick-Off in July, roughly a week before being told we had lost, the BigSoft CEO mentioned the great meeting he had had with the BigPharma CIO. He emphasized the importance of getting a deeper knowledge of our customers and a greater understanding of their needs! This was exactly what he had not done. He did not really care about the customer.
>
> You know, I'm not angry at BigPharma. I've met the new CEO at BigSoft, and I just can't believe a word he says. I just can't trust him."

Angela's story is completely true, even though obviously the names have been changed. It is a sad story. Angela had done everything right. Her product was a winner. She had tried to mitigate the risk of being a small company by partnering with BigSoft – but that was before they hired the new CEO. Angela had spent a long time building up trust with the CIO of BigPharma, but that was completely blown away in one foolhardy moment, by an arrogant ass.

Complete trust between people is infrequent, and between companies and individuals even more rare. Trust is not attainable by request or appeal and it is not transferrable. It has to be earned. Trust sits on the three pillars of authenticity, integrity and honesty; promising only what you can give, and giving what you promise. Attitude and preference, as they relate to how a customer thinks about your company, are as likely to be informed by whether a customer feels they can trust you as by the capabilities your company can provide.

However, in many cases, companies have defaulted on their obligations to customers, who feel ignored, poorly treated, and often perceive that their concerns as customers or consumers are rarely heard. I refer to this as the Trust Default.

Figure 6: Customers' Trust in Business

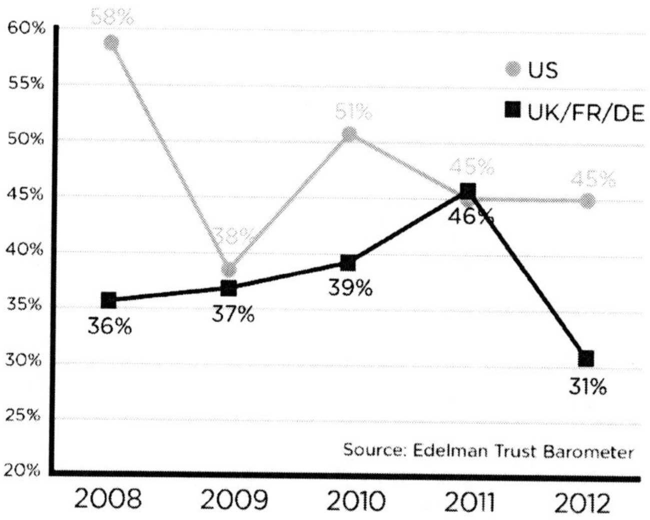

There is no question that trust in business has become more elusive. According to the 2012 Edelman Trust Barometer, just 45% of customers in the US trust businesses. In Europe, the situation is worse. Across the United Kingdom, France and Germany, less than one-third (31%) of customers feel they can trust business. The banking crisis and subsequent bailouts across the world have combined to infect industry in general, and financial services in particular, with a lingering malodorous tumor.

As a consequence of the Trust Default, developing trusted relationships with customers has never been more difficult. On the one hand the consequence of this is that the task of establishing true customer affinity might seem a little ambitious. But, on the other hand, if you are prepared to make the journey, you will find that not many others have joined you on the voyage. When you arrive at the destination you may well find that your only companion will be your customer.

From my perspective, what happened during the economic turmoil of the last decade was not so much a recession as a fundamental restructuring of the economic order. This is a good thing! It has forced us once more to focus on true difference *versus* positioned differentiation. To address the Trust Default, it has demanded a focus on values and ethics, underlining the value of trust as an asset.

We should recognize that, while honesty and integrity as propellants of commercial energy have not necessarily always been the most comfortable bedfellows with the pursuit of profit and revenue, what is scarce is valuable. If you are prepared to address the Trust Default, you have the opportunity to gain a considerable advantage over your competitors.

The Changing Shape of the Trust Circle

There was a time when people would look to figures of authority for advice and guidance. Government leaders and senior company executives were at the center of the Trust Circle and were considered a talisman for trust. It has been a while since that has been the case, and in recent times their trust bank has completely defaulted.

But nature abhors a vacuum and human nature dictates that we all have a deep yearning to trust and to be trusted. We now look elsewhere for credible sources or trusted advisors and, with increasing frequency, we are placing our trust in people like ourselves. We seek advice from people with whom we can relate, whose circumstances are similar to ours and who face the same challenges.

Independent research shows that the shape of the Trust Circle is changing. In compiling its excellent Trust Barometer, Edelman asked participants how credible they would consider information provided about a company from a variety of sources.

Figure 7: Who Do You Trust?

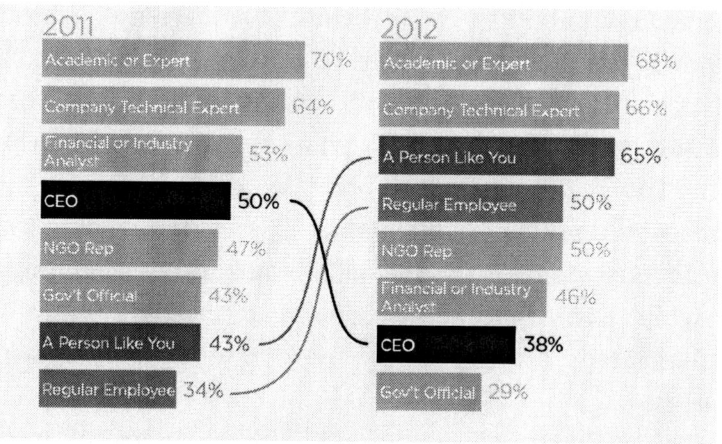

Between 2011 and 2012, CEOs and government officials plummeted on the credibility scale while peers and regular employees saw a dramatic rise. Customers trust your company's leadership far less than before. The customer needs to see you as 'A Person Like Me', someone who understands their world.

In many cases, CEOs only have themselves to blame. While professing to be customer-focused, they often are not sufficiently familiar with what the customer really wants, and even if they wanted to (which is rare in itself), they may not have the knowledge to effect the necessary change to deliver on the promises they unwisely make.

Building Trust

To develop a deep customer relationship you have to overcome the Trust Default. With the change in the shape of the Trust Circle you must accept that your customer's perception of you will gain less ground from your company's website or CEO pronouncements. You own this responsibility, and others will influence it.

If you are hoping to influence the customer's attitude towards you then you better be sure that what they hear about you from peers, academics, company technical experts, and the regular employees is what you would like them to hear. The reality is that what you, as a business, might broadcast in your public statements is of diminishing value. The actions you take and the value you add to the community in which you and your customer exist is what will fundamentally determine your reputation, and how you are perceived.

Here is what you need to do:

1. Invest your time to understand your customers' industry and their business. If you're to advise, you must be a subject matter expert.

2. You need to give value first and expect nothing in return. You are building a relationship for the long term, and it is only OK to ask for something from the customer when you've earned the right.
3. You need to be authentic, honest and fair – in everything, always.
4. You must focus on areas of Mutual Value, where what's good for the customer is also good for you – in that order. Explore the customer's Business Strategy, understand or suggest Business Initiatives to deliver on that strategy, and when you find an area that will make a real difference to the customer, see if you have a solution to their problem. Start with the problem, not the solution. If you discover that it is only good for you but not for the customer, then you should explain that to her and explore alternative approaches.
5. Choose your customers wisely, only applying the resources to customers for whom your products or services can truly deliver value. Don't try to force-fit your solution. It will only end up in tears.
6. Trust is a two-way street. If you are delivering on your promise, then it is only fair that the customer holds up her end of the bargain.
7. Recognize that some customers don't want this level of attention or relationship.
8. It boils down to value, and value propositions needs to be business-based, not feature-based, addressing the Critical Success Factors for key Business Initiatives. This means that you must first truly understand the customer's business.

9. Recognize that the impact on a customer of a bad buying decision is usually greater than the impact on you of a lost deal – and then act accordingly
10. Adopt the customer's perspective. Sit in the customer's chair and ask the question: "Would *I* buy from this company?" If you answer that question honestly, it will guide your actions.

Remember, customers don't need you to learn about your product: they can get all of the information they need from the Internet. They don't need you to recommend solutions: they can get that from their peers. Your opportunity is to help them shape their needs, identify or suggest initiatives, and then to figure out how you can apply your solutions to those initiatives. If you don't know how to do that you should look for outside assistance.

Trust is Personal

Lasting business relationships between the seller and the buyer, like lasting personal relationships, are built on a foundation of trust that for each of us is fundamentally personal. While always important, trust as a determining factor of business transaction efficacy increases or decreases in amplitude at different phases of the business interaction, because risk transfers from seller to buyer before and after the sale. Be conscious of that shift, bearing in mind that while you and your buyer may be engaged in a commercial interaction for your respective companies, trust is fundamentally personal.

Nothing Else Matters is a very personal song written by James Hetfield, singer and rhythm guitarist with the American heavy metal band Metallica. He wrote this song while he was on the phone with his then girlfriend. There are four lines in the song that go to the heart of establishing a trusted relationship:

Trust I seek and I find in you
Every day for us something new
Open mind for a different view
and nothing else matters.

Nothing Else Matters, Metallica, Metallica, 1992, reprinted with permission

If you want to be trusted by your customer, you will need to trust her first.

Now you can flip the Trust Default on its head. It should refer to the default position you take – a willingness to trust. If this is not currently your default approach, you will need an *open mind for a different view.* You may feel uncomfortable about this – but it is a major point that will deeply underpin your future success.

Trust is so important in developing long-term customer relationships that it is not too much of a stretch to say "… and nothing else matters." Thank you, James Hetfield.

CHAPTER 4

RESEARCH FOR INSIGHT

Value creation is one of the basic tenets upon which a successful sales career is built. For a salesperson to excel, he needs to understand his market and the unique advantage he brings his customer. He must develop a strategy to succeed, and then marshal the resources required to guarantee successful execution of his strategy. The superior sales professionals I have encountered view themselves as proprietors of their own businesses, concerning themselves with measurement of the value they deliver to their employers, their customers and themselves.

Selecting the right Accounts to serve, and the right Business Units within that Account are critical to achieving your revenue targets. Coupled with expression of the unique differentiated value that the customer cares about, this principle is at the core of effective Account Planning and can be the catalyst for unparalleled revenue acceleration in your own chosen marketplace.

Remember: your Account is a marketplace, and your goal is to be the leader in your market segment.

Account Planning is really strategic business planning applied on an individual customer basis. Pursuing this market (your customer) strategically is not the purview of the corporation, though many functions within your company have important roles to play; it belongs primarily in the hands of the Account Manager and the Account Team. After all, they spend more time with customers than anyone else.

Mutual Value is the desired destination you want to reach when building an Account Plan with, and for, your customer. Where investment by customer and supplier are truly aligned, there is an opportunity to create extraordinary value for both parties. If you fall on either side of the Mutual Value diagonal (**Figure 8**), one of you is losing out, investing more than you should, and not getting fair return.

Figure 8: The Mutual Value Chart

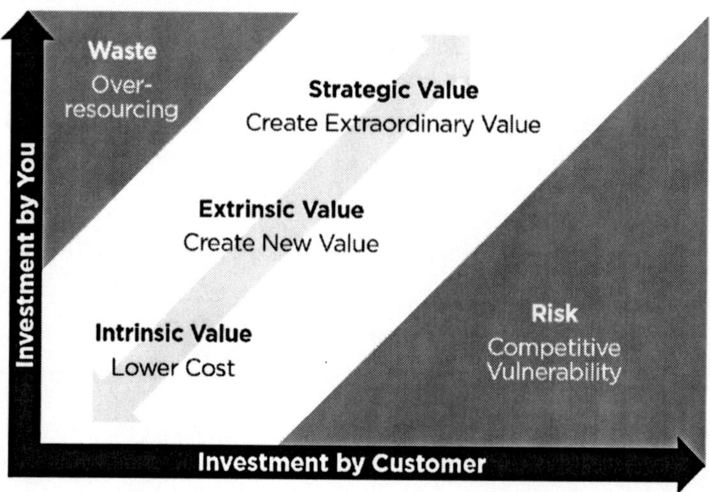

Before you can determine where the Mutual Value diagonal sits, you need to understand what is valuable to the customer. You probably know where you get value for your own products or services. To understand the customer's value filter you need to do your research, and that is the first step in Account Planning.

The Three Cs – Customer, Competitor, Company

As a user of Salesforce, you have a wealth of information stored in your CRM. This is where you record information about Accounts, Opportunities, Contacts, Competitors, Products, Tasks and Users (your Account Team members). As you build a picture of the Account (or Accounts) you are working on, you will need to use all of this information, as Salesforce will continue to be both the 'system of record', and also the engine that drives communication and collaboration.

In addition to this basic information, you also will need to understand the critical attributes of what I refer to as the *Three Cs: Customer, Competitor, Company*.

Later in this chapter, I will outline how you might begin to record and organize this information in Dealmaker Smart Account Manager in Salesforce. Maintaining a shared resource where everyone can access the information is critically important.

First I will review each of these information areas, focusing primarily on the Customer, and review what knowledge you might want to garner.

C #1 – The Customer

We start of course with the customer. You will recall from **CHAPTER 1: WHY ACCOUNT PLANNING MATTERS** that the reason you are developing the Account Plan is to *build long-term business relationships in a complex marketplace that enable you to create, develop, pursue, and win business that delivers mutual value.* That being the case, you need to understand that marketplace deeply. Here are the questions you should be able to answer about your customer's business.

Organization: How is the business organized? The organization is the physical implementation of the customer's business strategy. As a company develops its own go-to-market strategy, it will organize its physical structure to support that strategy. It is likely that there will be multiple channels to market, facilities in different countries, areas of specialty and focus, a high-level value proposition to each of its market segments, regional decision-making or centralized global policy-making. This is the landscape in which the customer operates every day, and you must understand the patterns in the fabric of its organizational design so that you can weave it into the tapestry of your plan.

Buying Process: As macro-economic factors evolve, so too does the buying process in an Account. In most cases large businesses have a buying process – a procedure that is generally followed for all, or most, major business purchases. The complexity of the buying process is usually linked to the size of the deal. Bigger deals present greater risk for the customer, and consequently attract significantly more diligence in the process. Incumbent suppliers already have scaled certain heights for the customer and have had the opportunity to establish credibility and relationship with the buyer. It is frequently much harder for a company to purchase from a vendor who is not already an approved supplier, and so customers stick with their existing suppliers if they can show sustained performance.

There is sometimes a 'perspective gap' between the buying community and the selling community. Professional buyers know every step they want to take in the buying cycle. They have a detailed project plan. There are hurdles and obstacles you have to scale. Unless you can visualize the route they want to take, and you have your own map to get there, guiding them to your chosen destination, you won't be with them when they reach their journey's end.

People: Trying to understand who the Key Players are in a large corporation is sometimes a bit like a Broadway production. Does the play have a cast of thousands or is it a one-man show? Who is playing what role? Who is the lead? How important is the supporting cast? Who are the star players? Is it the Chief Financial Officer who controls the money, or the CIO who sets the technology standards for the company? Is the Director of Purchasing, who manages the Preferred Vendor list, in a cameo role, or is he really the star attraction? Maybe the star is the Vice President of Sales who has the business problem, or the sales person who will end up using the product. People issues that are important in an opportunity exist in a different way in an account, as you are setting the stage more often than closing the play. In either case, you need to know your lines.

I will describe later in **CHAPTER 8: ACCESSING KEY PLAYERS** how to identify Key Players in the organization and their purpose in Account Planning. I will show how to place each of the players into the Inner Circle, Political Structure, or Outside Political Structure, each respectively having roles to control outcomes, make things happen, or watch and wonder.

Business Units and Service Units: All large companies have many discrete functional departments and multiple divisions. Not all are created equal, and you will need to know their relative importance. I will describe how to prioritize these in **CHAPTER 6: SEGMENT FOR PRIORITY**, but you can begin to illuminate the differences by identifying Business Units and Service Units.

Business Units manage the primary customer-facing activity of the company. They are a fundamental unit of planning and investment, measured and managed as a source of profit and loss, offering defined products and services, targeted to specific external markets. Strategic decisions are made here.

Service Units, as the name suggests, work internally to serve the Business Units. They are measured and managed as cost centers by the enterprise, serving internal markets, and can be centralized or decentralized. Service Units are frequently subject to budget cuts and / or outsourcing.

Business Units typically strive for competitive advantage and growth and you need to help them create value. Service Units, on the other hand, such as the Procurement Department, usually look to lower prices as the driving force behind their purchases.

Customer Relationship: A key element of the research you need to undertake pertains to the relationship between your company and the target account. When your customers think about you (if they think about you at all), what phrase do you think comes to mind? Is it *Vendor, Credible Source,* or *Problem Solver,* or are you possibly the sun around which their strategic planets revolve – the apogee of business relationships – the *Trusted Advisor*? Trusted Advisors form a true partnership with their customers and develop significant Mutual Value – and that's what Account Planning and Management is all about.

It's always good to be the Trusted Advisor right? No one wants to be 'just' a Vendor. Well, that's not always true. There is no right and wrong – the level of relationship needs to be appropriate to the business opportunity and reflect the customer's commitment – and as you traverse the different Business Units within an account, the appropriate level of relationship may well vary. Once you understand what level of relationship is apposite to the opportunity in the Account, you will need to evaluate the relationship that you have and address the relationship gap.

You must carefully select the customers, or the areas within a Large Account where the opportunity merits significant investment. I will explore the methodology behind this task in **CHAPTER 6: SEGMENT FOR PRIORITY**. When you identify that rich opportunity source, your understanding of the drivers that move and shape the business will help you to raise your level of relationship.

Customer Ecosystem: Companies are like organic beings, influenced by the environment in which they exist. They grow and evolve in response to internal and external stimuli, and generally it is these stimuli that inform a company's Goals, Business Drivers and Business Initiatives. Remember that you are still in research mode. As you augment your appreciation for the elements in their environment, you will be better positioned to enhance the value that you can provide.

Who are their customers, competitors, suppliers and business partners? What external or internal stimuli are causing them to act? Are there advancements in the technological landscape in their marketplace that are driving them to change? Do they need to react to mergers and acquisitions (M&A) activity in the market? Is it impacting their relative market position? What financial, operational, or regulatory challenges do they have to address? What are the macro-trends in their industry? Is their market growing or declining?

A thorough understanding of the Customer Ecosystem will guide you to shape your own interactions with the customer and then to share your expertise in areas where you might be able to assist. Of course your research may uncover incompatibilities of which you were unaware, or you may discover that the opportunity is too small to merit the significant effort that is involved in the pursuit of a Large Account. If so, it is always better to determine this early.

When you have established that you are focused on the right account, it is worth doing as much research as possible to identify the Business Drivers that are attracting most attention in each of your selected Business and Service Units. Some may be common across the account, but dig a little deeper to get to the core issues for each unit.

C #2 – The Competitor

When you lose a deal to a competitor in one of your key Accounts, not only have you lost the deal, the competitor also has grown in strength in the Account. Losing a deal is not an isolated event; it ripples through all of your efforts and weakens your position in the Account. It is not a good thing.

Stiff competition
All over the world

Stiff Competition, Heaven Tonight, Cheap Trick, 1978

In the context of Account Planning, I define 'competition' as:

> ... any alternative force, internal or external, that prevents you from achieving your goals and objectives.

Competitors can come in many forms: external companies looking to be the selected supplier; the customer preferring to Do Nothing and maintain the *status quo*; or internal suppliers such as a Service Unit in the customer's organization. In all cases, you should consider how to compete with them and be prepared to articulate your unique competitive advantage. To do so you will need to know your competitors well.

Strengths and Weaknesses: Do yourself a favor, and make sure that you list two strengths of your competitor for every single competitor weakness. It is usually pretty easy to come up with reasons why you're better than the competitor, but you should know that already. Remember you are dealing with Account Planning, so in addition to the Product / Services / Capabilities referenced below, you will want to think about the reasons from the customer's perspective as to why they will choose to do business with your competitor, or what they may perceive as a basis to not support them. Value arrives when you can come up with reasons why the competitor is better than you in the eyes of the customer, and then figure out how to overcome their competitive advantage.

Products / Services / Capabilities: In the context of what you expect the Account will require (acknowledging that you must make some assumptions when you are early in the process), what standard offerings are available from the competitor, and what capabilities do they have to extend or modify their product or service to meet the customer's needs?

It is important to consider the 'whole product' and not just the 'basic product'. For example, if you have a technically superior product to your competitor, but the competitor has a global support infrastructure that is superior to yours, the customer might consider the competitor's 'whole product' to be better, or more complete.

On the other hand, if your software product sale is likely to face competition from the internal IT department (a Service Unit), which typically wants to build a customer software solution, it is quite likely that cost will be one of their competitive arguments. This is often the case in a 'build *versus* buy' decision. However, it may well be that your business buyer will recognize the 'whole product' solution including ongoing enhancement, technical support infrastructure, etc, as a compelling reason to consider your offering.

When assessing your competitors' products or services, you must adopt your customer's perspective and consider not just the features or specifications, but the overall solution as it can be applied to solve the customer's 'whole problem.'

Positioning: When Marc Benioff introduced salesforce.com to the world, he was very clear on how he positioned the company. "No Software" was the mantra frequently and consistently heard in downtown San Francisco. At the same time he positioned Oracle and SAP as old-fashioned, expensive and lacking in innovation by re-defining the CRM landscape.

There is a (possibly apocryphal) story about a comment made by Marc Benioff at salesforce.com's Dreamforce event in 2005. Oracle's announcement of the Siebel acquisition coincided with Dreamforce, and it is said that Benioff referred to the combined entity as "a one-stop-shop for obsolescence." I was at Dreamforce that year, and I did not hear that comment during any of the main sessions, so the veracity of the story is a little uncertain. What is certain however is that, as salesforce.com positioned itself in the eyes of its customers, it also positioned its competitors.

When in 2005 we started our journey to leverage technology (Dealmaker) to fundamentally change the sales training industry, we presented a view that effective adoption of sales methodology could happen only when supported by intelligent software integrated with CRM. The traditional sales training providers reared up as one, belittling the value of technology in sales training and dismissing us as irrelevant. Our competitors positioned us as solely focused on technology with (by implication) weak sales methodology, even though we had one of the largest research teams in the business. Thankfully their positioning did not work and we were repeatedly recognized as leaders in our industry. The point remains though that, as evidenced by this and the salesforce.com story above, positioning happens.

As you research your competitors, you should reflect on how they position themselves and how they position you, and be prepared yourself to tell your story. That way the customer will be able to imagine the future through the prism of your perspective.

History and Relationship: It is always very difficult to compete with an incumbent supplier that has a good relationship with the customer. On the other hand, most companies go though purchasing cycles that require a review of their suppliers on a frequent basis. To develop an effective strategy for the Account, as part of your Account Plan, you will need to know what the customer has purchased from the competitor in that past. You also should look for information that can guide you to assess the level of relationship that the competitor has with the Key Players in the business.

C #3 – Your Company

This should be the easy one. Of course you need to be fully conversant in your own company's products, services, and capabilities, and most importantly the proven value that you have delivered to other customers. To marshal the internal resources that you will need to deliver on your plan, you will have to be crystal clear on the strategic imperatives that are driving the business. As you develop your Account Plan you are looking for areas of Mutual Value. This will only occur if you understand what is valuable to your business. As you get into **CHAPTER 6: SEGMENT FOR PRIORITY**, you must have a good appreciation of what an attractive market segment looks like so that you can prioritize accordingly. Similarly, when you get to selecting which opportunities to target using the Value Map (**CHAPTER 9: FOCUS FOR IMPACT**) the determinants of *Value to Us* will guide the selection to ensure that this is where your efforts ought to be applied.

Let's now look at how you might capture and record the information pertaining to the Three Cs in a structured manner within Salesforce.

Building your Account Plan in Salesforce

Dealmaker Smart Account Manager is the recommended Account Planning and Management solution for users of Salesforce. It applies automation and intelligence so it is easy to adopt Account Planning and Management as part of your company's processes. It is not the only option available, but it is the one that salesforce.com has chosen for its own Account Planning efforts, and is of course the one that I am most familiar with.

Plan Details in Dealmaker Smart Account Manager is the area where you record the background information and research on the Account(s) in your Account Plan, as well as monitor the progress through the development of your plan.

Plan Details is a set of 21 information areas or questions, grouped into four sections that map your progress through your Account Planning and Execution. Plan Details can be used as an outline of the plan information and as an indicator of the level of plan completion. **Figure 9** shows a summary view of Plan Details.

Dealmaker Smart Account Manager comes pre-configured with section headings, questions and values for the responses to each question, and can be configured for your business if you require different sections or questions.

Whether you choose to use Dealmaker or not, you might use the following 21 elements to begin to build a picture of your account, develop a roadmap for your Account Planning and Management activities, and provide a quick summary to review with your customer, your Account Team, and your management.

Figure 9: Plan Details – Summary View

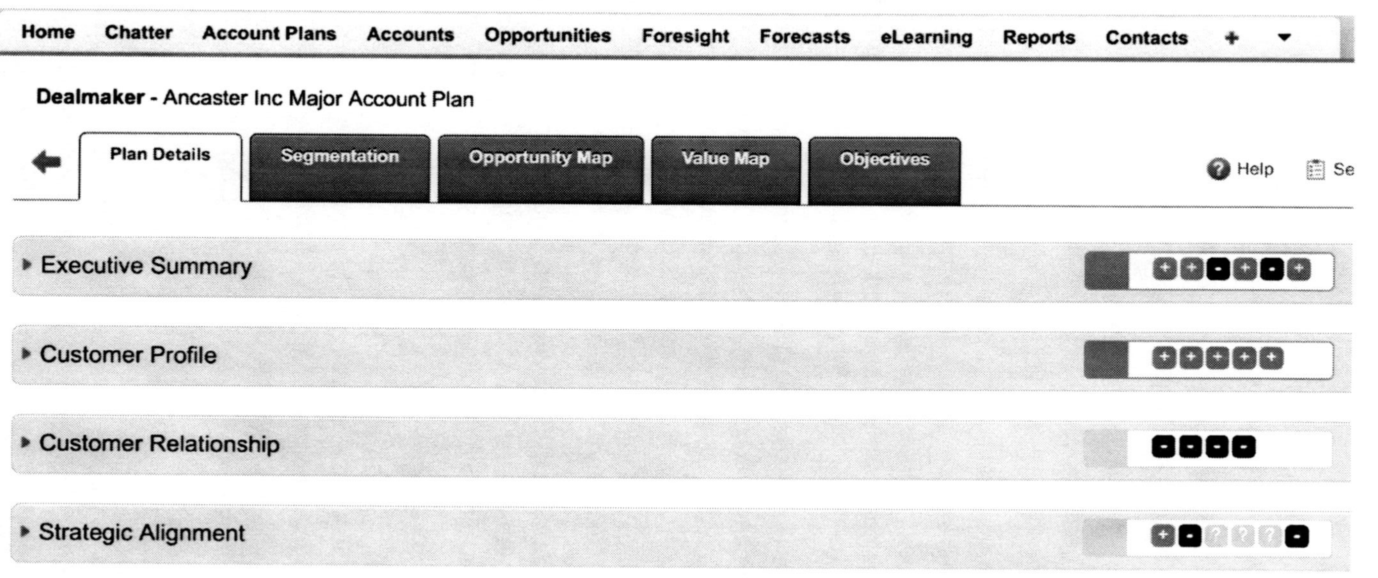

Executive Summary: A summary description of the current business environment for the Account or Accounts (your marketplace) in your plan.

Revenue Target: The revenue to be achieved in the plan period from the Account or Accounts in the plan.

Historical Business: A description of the historical purchase behavior of the Account, including revenue and product and/or services.

Overall Account Goal: A broad statement that defines your desired state with your Account at the end of the plan period. Your business development, revenue, and cross-account objectives should support your Account Goal and be included here as part of the description.

Resource Requirements: People, departments, groups, team members, executives, programs, initiatives in your organization that are needed to achieve your Objectives and Account Goals. Resources outside your organization – such as partners or other customers – also should be included if necessary for the success of the plan.

Critical Success Factors: The critical activities you need to take in order to successfully implement your plan. These are activities which, if missed, would cause your plan to fail.

Customer Business: Description (and suitability assessment) of the customer's business, their industry, market and company size, as well as their high-level Goals, Business Drivers (internal and external pressures) and Business Initiatives. You are looking to assess the suitability of this customer for you, and their fit in your 'sweet spot' or target market.

Business and Service Units: Accounts and their corresponding Business or Service Units selected for this plan, including a description and location of each unit.

Customer Financial Condition: Revenue, cash, profit and investment trends, comparison with similar companies, and performance against key performance metrics. (Positive means that their financial condition is compatible with Business Initiatives.)

Customer Industry Trends: Factors that indicate whether this is a growing, mature or declining market, changes in the competitive landscape, demographic or geographic shifts, and macro-economic, technology-based, or other pressures.

Technology / Regulatory / Environmental Landscape: The specific characteristics or elements in the Account's operations that are most relevant to the solutions you plan to position or have currently implemented within the Account.

The Customer's Perception of Your Company: The Account's overall perception of your reputation and the value you bring to the market.

Cultural Compatibility: The extent to which the customer's culture resembles that of your company, exhibited by how it operates its business and its behaviors, practices and values.

Executive Credibility: Level of relationship and access to the senior executives who are in the Inner Circle or Political Structure when deciding which providers (Vendors) they will invest with, as it relates to a strategic relationship for this Account.

Customer Satisfaction: The customer satisfaction score or rating based on customer satisfaction surveys conducted with the customer OR your understanding of the customer's satisfaction with your solutions and service.

Customer Business Priorities: The areas of focus, confirmed by the customer, that are deemed essential to the health of the business. The priorities typically will be in response to financial, operational, competitive, or other internal or external pressures (Business Drivers) that are compelling the customer to act.

Your Strategic Initiatives for the Customer: Your solutions or initiatives that you would like to position with the customer in response to the customer's business priorities.

Reference Cases: Customer success stories with business results that support the strategic initiatives you plan to position with the customer.

Value Proposition: A promise of value, which can be articulated consistently by all of the Account Team, to be delivered such that it engenders a belief from the customer that value will be experienced.

Solution Vision (Presentation / Prototype): A demonstration or proof of concept or illustration of your proposed solution that aligns to your value proposition, and your strategic initiatives to meet the customer's business priorities.

Customer Alignment: Customer's confirmation that execution of the plan will deliver positive impact in line with the customer's Business Priorities.

Think about the kind of information needed as you build your foundation, and use this framework as a guideline. Doing this part of the task well will save you countless hours in the future, and help establish immediate credibility for you when you do begin to interact with the customer. It just takes initiative – and just a little bit of – you've guessed it – research. That's where you get the insight.

CHAPTER 5

INTEGRATE FOR VELOCITY

Albert Einstein's father, Hermann Einstein, was a salesman and engineer. Hermann, born 1847, spent the majority of his working life building and selling dynamos and electrical meters that were based on direct electrical current (DC). In the true spirit of salesmen everywhere, always looking for a party, Hermann's company was the first to provide lights to illuminate Oktoberfest. That was in 1885. He subsequently lost a bidding war for the electrification contract of Munich to Siemens, which promoted the modern alternating current (AC). Siemens is a Dealmaker and TAS customer – although I don't think they were at that time. Funny thing – I am an engineer, a CEO, and a sales person – perhaps I've found my role model!

When Albert Einstein wrote the best-known mathematical formula of all time (the mass-energy equivalence formula $E=mc^2$, where E is energy, m is mass and c is velocity), it may not have been a coincidence that velocity is the factor that is squared, having more impact on the equivalence than either energy or mass. A small change in velocity and *poof!* the laws of physics kick in and energy and mass are severely impacted. Velocity matters. Albert said so.

But are things moving too quickly for you? Do you ever have one of those days when you get up and hope that – just for one day – nothing changes? Sometimes it feels as if you are barely hanging on, buffeted by a torrent of innovation and evolution. But maybe today will be the day when you won't have to adjust or adapt, reorganize or rework ... But, I don't think so.

Things are happening more quickly than ever. I am writing this in late 2012, and in the next 30 minutes or so:

- 700,000 apps will be downloaded from the AppStore.
- 56 million 'likes' will be added on Facebook.
- There will be 500,000 visitors to LinkedIn.
- 6 billion emails will be sent.
- YouTube will show 90 million videos and 1,800 hours of new video will be uploaded.
- 500,000 hours will be spent by people watching movies on Netflix.
- 5 million tweets will be posted to Twitter.
- Users will spend 146 days on Facebook – yes, in the next 30 minutes – think about that.
- 350,000 people will visit Pinterest.
- 5 million photos will be added to Facebook.
- 21,000 new Twitter accounts will be created.

Many of these examples are consumer-oriented, and you may consider them less relevant to commerce in the B2B arena. However, I think anyone who operates in the business world should take note of these trends. People's attitudes as business buyers or sellers are shaped by what they learn as consumers. There is a metamorphosis of human interaction that you can witness first-hand. If you observe carefully, you will see that consumers are often the first to travel the journey that businesses subsequently follow.

Consider the changes you've seen in business over the past 10 years – particularly when it comes to technology – and notice that consumer behavior is always a good indicator of what will happen in the business world. Trends that you see in B2C interactions are usually followed by similar engagement in the B2B world.

As an example: consumers were the first players in the 'app economy,' downloading applications from Apple's AppStore, only to be followed by businesses that are now both distributing and consuming applications in this self-service model. In the software world, online application stores from new-economy players – such as the AppExchange from salesforce.com, and Google's Marketplace – now sit alongside offerings from the traditional software companies. SAP provides the Ecohub that it describes as "the community-powered online solution marketplace that is your trusted source for discovering, evaluating, and buying solutions from SAP." Microsoft – which for a long time might have been accused of fighting the subscription economy – now has its own Marketplace that, as of October 2012, provided 125,000 apps.

In the online economy SAP and Microsoft, which formerly were committed to a traditional business model, have morphed their offerings to mimic consumer interactions, a model more comfortable for salesforce.com and Google, and, of course, for Amazon. Amazon has evolved its consumer online store into a full business solution with Amazon Web Services. HP's Storefront Portal and Oracle's Digital Store are two more examples of business reflecting consumer trends.

It is not so much the consumerization of technology, because most consumers care little about the developments I've described here, but businesses now are developing approaches that model how consumers behave in their buying interactions – so that buyers can adopt patterns of behavior with which they have subconsciously become familiar.

Think about this: not all consumers are B2B buyers, but all B2B buyers are consumers.

As if by osmosis, people are conditioned to new ways of thinking about the interactions they have as consumers, and begin to expect similar capability or convenience in their business connections and interplays. And it happens without anyone noticing: incremental changes in behavior and expectation, satisfaction and dissatisfaction.

The fact remains that all business people – both sellers and buyers – are consumers, and the lessons they learn in 'consumer-land' shape their thinking and expectations in 'business-land.' Just think about what happened to Research in Motion – the makers of the once irreplaceable Blackberry.

Consumers, salespeople and B2B buyers are changing, and not just in a small way. It's almost as if there is a remodeling or metamorphosis of the rules of both intrinsic and extrinsic behaviors before our eyes. If you take the time to step back for a minute, you can observe continuous evolution. It is evident in how people connect, communicate, and collaborate; their quest for visible progress and feedback; their limited attention span; changing personal motivations; unusually peripatetic career paths; a desire for increased autonomy and self-mastery; actions more redolent of entrepreneurialism than traditional workplace obedience; a preference for where and how they work; an expectation or demand for an array of tools to apply; an acceptance of disruption and interruption; and a predilection to disrupt and interrupt.

When you place these developments alongside the seemingly inexorable march of mobile devices as the primary force in business interactions, the velocity at which people interact is evidentially a paradigm that must be considered in any business plan.

There are now approximately 6.5 billion mobile subscribers in the world, and mobile infrastructure spend, already at more than $55bn in 2012, is expected to grow to $68bn in 2016. Everyone is connected, always on, all of the time. No-one waits for information anymore: they are browsing, Googling, or asking Siri, constantly tethered and plugged into a growing and connected economic and social ecosystem.

If you're hoping that today will be the day that the landscape in which you operate doesn't change, then I expect you are out of luck. You might hope for a respite to give you time to catch your breath, or you may rail against the torrent of technological advancement, or perhaps you will seek to deflect the buffeting winds of rapid change. It is unlikely that such approaches will serve you well.

On the other hand, you could choose to embrace the change, and be part of it, seeking new ways to do the tasks that are perhaps mundane or not operating optimally, and then – and here is the exciting part – you might find that there are new opportunities emerging that you never thought possible. Such is the case with Account Planning.

When Account Planning Goes Bad

When things move at the velocity outlined above, and where business customers have been conditioned to act like impatient consumers, bad things happen if you have not put a communication, collaboration, and response system in place that meets their expectations.

Think about your largest customer and the most important opportunity that you are working on with them today. If you just now received a call, or more likely an email, to inform you that you had lost the sale, and that the customer is inviting your largest competitor to 'partner' with them in the Account, I think you would be pretty upset. But could you list the three most likely reasons why that happened? Go on. Give it a go.

1. ______________________________
2. ______________________________
3. ______________________________

Until a deal is closed, there is always risk. If you can't list the three reasons, then I'd suggest that you're possibly in denial, or someone has not communicated effectively with you. On the other hand, if you can list the risks, then shouldn't you be doing something about them – before you get the call?

When reviewing sales opportunities I call the reason why a deal might be lost the 'Critical Risk.' But when managing a Large Account, I refer to it as the 'Super Critical Risk.' The downside is enormous. Foreseeing this risk, and resolving it quickly before you get the call, is important.

Large Account Planning and Management is complex. Consider the multiplicative effect of (1) what you are selling – a number of solutions; (2) where you are selling – many geographic locations, each potentially with multiple business units; (3) who is selling – each solution and location is potentially being touched by different members of your Account Team; and that is before considering (4) the customer, the people in the customer's organization that we need to collaborate with in developing the plan, or the people we need to influence in executing on the plan. Oh, wait, I forgot about (5) the executive management in your company who review and monitor the plan.

There are lots of people. There are numerous opportunities for failure, and too many potential Super Critical Risks.

Time is rarely your friend in sales. Sales opportunities are always moving forwards or backwards – things never stay the same. Because of the ubiquity of the Internet and pace of information flow through online social networks, your customers are constantly learning about how to solve the problems they face. If you are not on top of things, communicating frequently and promptly, then you are leaving space for your competitors to fill.

Finding the time to complete your plan, and then keeping the plan alive and constantly updated, while engaging your Account Team members, and your customer, can be a daunting challenge. All too frequently, plans are developed at a point in time, and then left to gather dust on the shelf until next year's planning time comes around.

The efficacy of your Account Planning efforts is a function of the completeness of the plan, the engagement with the customer, the involvement of your whole team, and the cadence of action and updates. Efficiency is of the essence in developing the plan, and constant communication is paramount in keeping the plan alive. There is only one way to do that, and that is to integrate Account Planning and

Management into both the systems you use today and the daily workflow of the Account Team.

This is where you should use your Salesforce CRM to help as the foundation for your integrated Account Planning and Management system.

Integrate for Velocity

There are four primary sources of input to your Account Plan and you will benefit hugely if you can integrate them. They are:

- Existing CRM data in Salesforce.
- Knowledge of the Account Team.
- Information shared by the customer.
- Supplementary data from research sources, such as Data.com.

Before discussing how these sources should be brought together in one integrated approach, we should take a moment to consider where Account Planning sits in the overall spectrum of managing the business of sales. You might consider the cadence shown in **Figure 10**.

Most companies do some form of Territory Planning annually to arrange their go-to-market strategy. When focus shifts to deals or individual transactions, Opportunity Planning becomes part of the sales operational plan, its frequency driven by the profile of the typical sales opportunity being pursued by each go-to-market channel and its consequent sales-cycle.

Figure 10: The Account Plan Spectrum

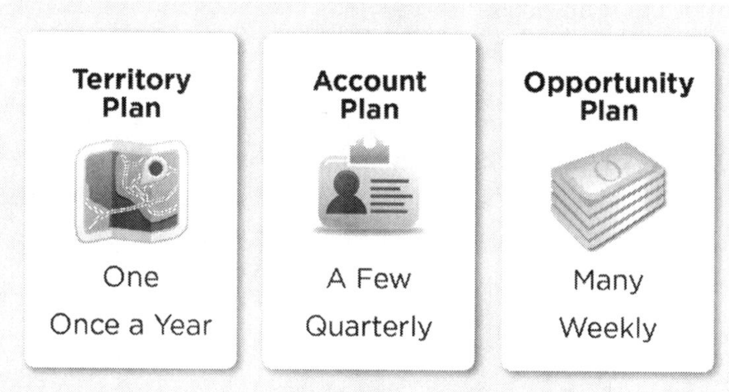

As your company moves through its own lifecycle you earn the right to ask for bigger pieces of business, particularly from your larger customers. That is when you need to recognize the necessity to operationalize Account Planning, sitting between your Territory Planning and your Opportunity Planning.

> Note: You may be forgiven for thinking at this stage that Account Planning only applies when you are working on very large Accounts. But remember you are working with the concept of a marketplace. In place of the many divisions in a large organization, your market might consist of a number of smaller Accounts in your territory. I refer to this as 'Portfolio Planning' and the majority of the principles I relate in this book apply equally well to a portfolio of Accounts.

Account Planning gives a longer time-horizon than Opportunity Planning, and typically starts at the higher end of the business, where for example you might be involved in pursuing Fortune 500 complex organizations.

In the case of salesforce.com, Account Planning started with the Enterprise division, and then rippled down to the mid-market and on into the SMB market in the top part of that tier. Salesforce.com is offering a broader set of products today than when it started doing business, and the smart people at One Landmark recognized that they would benefit from the discipline of Account Planning, understanding that it would provide a hastened ability to penetrate more deeply into its customers.

Account Plans are created not only for the sales person and her manager, they should also serve the business oversight and strategy requirements of the company's executives. The sales person or Account Manager and her Account Team are concerned primarily with learning about the Account to discover value, and to execute on the plan, but it is important to recognize that it doesn't stop there.

You are writing the Account Plan, not just for yourself and your customer, but also for all of the contributors in your internal organization who you will call on to support you in the process, and who likely will want to review what you are doing and to monitor progress.

As salesforce.com embarked on Account Planning, in parallel to the pursuit of larger deals from larger customers, the opportunity scope grew, as did the complexity of the engagement. That meant that there were more players who had roles to perform in the overall production. In some cases, for some of salesforce.com's largest deals, up to 150 salesforce.com individuals were involved. So, the need for communication among the Account Team, each of the supporting players, and of course the executives who were reviewing the plans, monitoring performance and getting involved in closing the large deals, it was critical.

Figure 11: The Account Plan – for Reps, Managers and Executives

Without a centralized way to manage the plan, velocity and effectiveness suffer. When a product specialist or executive is called on to support the engagement with a large account, the quickest way for them to understand what the customer does, what they are focused on as a business, where you are in the account, and what issues you are looking to address, is to review a well-structured Account Plan. That way you align everyone to face the same direction, deliver the same messages, and present a cohesive strategy.

Do It All in Salesforce

You know that Salesforce is a great place to store, share and collaborate on the information you need to run your business. Within the Sales Cloud you get all the CRM capabilities you'd expect from Salesforce, to grow revenue, boost productivity, and get visibility into your business. It makes sense to me that this is where you would integrate your Account Planning framework and extend the capabilities of your CRM to support your work with Large Accounts.

Let's consider again the four sources of input that you might want to consider as part of your integrated solution. Here I will use Dealmaker Smart Account Manager to show what an integrated solution might look like, though you can use another approach. Just be sure that your combined data, knowledge and information are all integrated with Salesforce to achieve the effectiveness and velocity that you require.

CRM Data: In most cases much of the data you need already resides in your Salesforce CRM system. This is where you have recorded your account structure, your open and closed opportunities, account history, customer communications, internal discussions, and all of the detail on the key contacts in the organization. It is not all you need to do effective Account Planning, but it is really a great place to start. I can't think of any good reason why it doesn't make absolute sense to try to leverage that resource – automatically.

Figure 12 shows an Opportunity Map in Dealmaker Smart Account Manager. Dealmaker runs natively on the Force.com platform, in the Sales Cloud, leveraging and extending the Salesforce data model so you get the ultimate in resource and data sharing within the Salesforce security model.

Figure 12: The Opportunity Map

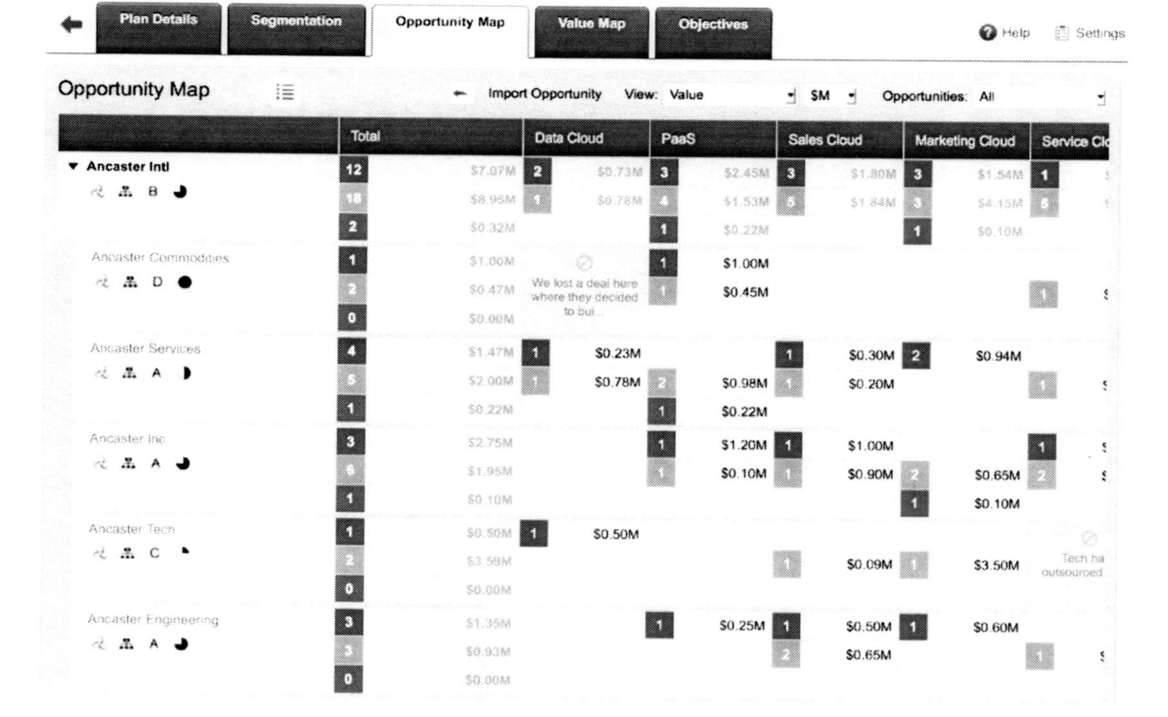

Plan Details
Segmentation
Opportunity Map
Value Map
Objectives
Help
Settings
Opportunity Map
Import Opportunity
View: Value
$M
Opportunities: All
Total
Data Cloud
PaaS
Sales Cloud
Marketing Cloud
Ancaster Intl
Ancaster Commodities
We lost a deal here where they decided to bui...
Ancaster Services
Ancaster Inc
Ancaster Tech
Ancaster Engineering

There are three main areas on the Opportunity Map:

- **Solutions:** Dealmaker Smart Account Manager maintains in Salesforce a list of all the Solutions you sell. It is then easy to place these solutions on your Opportunity Map. The columns on the map (shown as PaaS, Sales Cloud, Marketing Cloud, and Service Cloud in this example) represent the solutions you are selling to the account. Later you will see how to record opportunities against each of the Solutions.
- **Plan Units:** An Account Plan can cater for one or more Accounts. When dealing with large companies, frequently you will have more than one Account Record in Salesforce relevant to the Account Plan. In this example for Ancaster International, the individual Account units are shown as Ancaster Services, Ancaster Commodities, Ancaster Inc, Ancaster Tech and Ancaster Engineering.

  Imagine that you are the Account Manager for your company for HP. In Salesforce, you will likely have multiple Account Records for each of HP's business divisions. The Account Plan is where you pull all of these together. Dealmaker uses the Account Records in the CRM to populate the Opportunity Map. Anytime you add a new Account Record or contact to the Account, Dealmaker can see it automatically. Compare the velocity you can achieve doing it that way rather than trying to use PowerPoint to maintain an up-to-date picture of an organization as complex as HP.
- **Opportunities:** Your goal is to identify, create, and win opportunities at each intersection of the Solutions and Plan Units. When building your Account Plan, it is

always good to start with a picture of the current state. What opportunities are already closed? What opportunities are you currently working on? These opportunities already exist in the CRM, and Dealmaker uses the Salesforce data to build your starting position, and to inform future updates. As you work the plan, you will add more opportunities and perhaps assign tasks to Account Team members. Tasks are fully integrated with your Task List, and the Account Team members are selected from the list of users in your Salesforce system. Maintaining this tight integration delivers efficiencies in the development and maintenance of the plan and allows you to spend your valuable time in creating value for the customer.

Supplementary Data: To augment your core CRM data, you need to do research. (This is very important and I address it fully in **CHAPTER 4: RESEARCH FOR INSIGHT**). If you choose to use a third party business data provider to help with this task, there are a number of providers out there. As a salesforce.com customer, you will be aware of Data.com. While there are other solutions available, Data.com is a great example of where you might look for the supplementary data that you need, primarily because it is completely integrated with Salesforce. The more integrated you can make your complete Account Planning and Management system, the more you can protect the integrity of your data and processes, and the greater velocity you will achieve. Coupled with that, the 200 million company profiles from D&B and 30 million complete contacts from Jigsaw make Data.com a front-runner.

In **Figure 13** you can see the kind of supplementary data you might want to begin recording in your Account Plan.

Figure 13: Plan Details – Detailed View

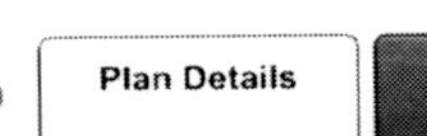
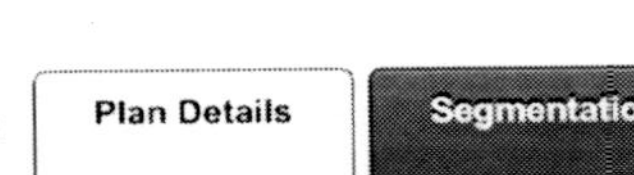

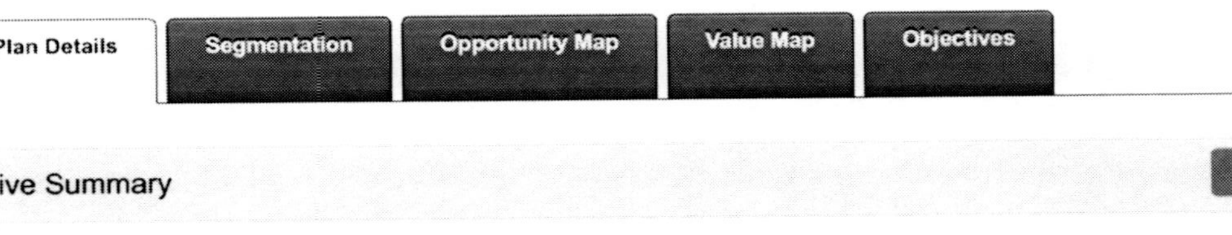

Customer Profile
7 Customer Business
+ Strong
Operating in the Telco Engineering Market, the majority of the revenue (68%) is in North America, followed by EMEA (22%) and APAC (10%). New entrant Hazard Wire Inc. is strong in APAC. New regulations and demand for wireless spectrum are high on the agenda.

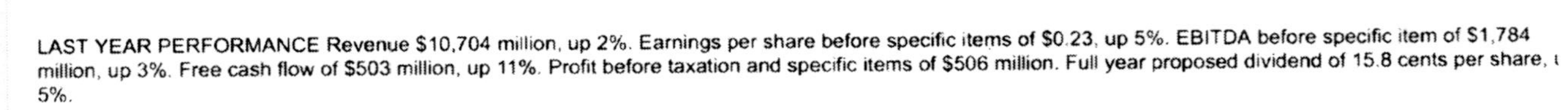

9 Customer Financial Condition
+ Positive
LAST YEAR PERFORMANCE Revenue $10,704 million, up 2%. Earnings per share before specific items of $0.23, up 5%. EBITDA before specific item of $1,784 million, up 3%. Free cash flow of $503 million, up 11%. Profit before taxation and specific items of $506 million. Full year proposed dividend of 15.8 cents per share,
5%.

In **CHAPTER 4: RESEARCH FOR INSIGHT**, I list the research that you may want to complete as you build your plan. One of the sections relates to *Customer Profile*, and as you can see in **Figure 13**, this is a great place to capture (manually or programmatically) the information from Data.com as it relates to *Customer Business Profile, Company Structure,* and *Customer Financial Condition*.

Knowledge of the (Whole) Team: You know that Account Planning is a team sport. Each of your Account Team members need to be able to contribute the knowledge they have and constantly update the plan as they acquire new pieces of knowledge. All other team members will benefit if they receive these updates in real time. Making your Account Plan easy to share with your team members during both the planning and execution phases delivers uncommon organizational velocity. This is the third important integration component – the integration of your *whole* team. Remember that the Account Plan is your roadmap for success in the Account and everyone on the team needs to know which direction to take.

Integrating your Account Plan in Salesforce is the best way to leverage all of the assets of your company, not just the formal Account Team. Perhaps there is a role for the product management function to share your company's product roadmap with the customer. There is surely assistance you can get from your marketing colleagues. If you need partners to complement the services you provide, you could turn to your business development or strategic alliances team. Get your workmates over in the finance department involved – I know you have friends who are accountants – they can help you analyze the financial benefit you expect to deliver to the customer through your plan. You might even have them meet their counterpart in the customer's organization – it would be good for them to get out!

But, seriously, integrate all of the relevant resources in your company to keep things moving quickly. They do want to help.

Information from the Customer: The most important constituency that contributes to the success of your plan is the customer. The information they share is the foundation on which each of the other pillars stands.

You can learn about the customer's Goals, Business Drivers, Customer Initiatives and Critical Success Factors only from her. I recommend building a Strategy Map (as shown in **Figure 14**) with the customer to involve her in the process and to confirm that your understanding of her business is complete. As with all elements of the Account Plan, the Strategy Map is attached to the plan and, as part of the plan, is attached to the Account Record in Salesforce.

Once you have the information, it is critical that you share it with all Account Team members. Dealmaker will follow all of the account sharing rules in Salesforce so that everyone who is supposed to see the plan can do so. Together, you can work to devise the correct approach to guide the customer to validate that the plan you have developed will deliver the impact that she needs.

Later in **CHAPTER 7: PEOPLE AND PROBLEMS**, I will go into detail on how you apply solid Account Planning methodology to this aspect of the task.

Figure 14: The Strategy Map

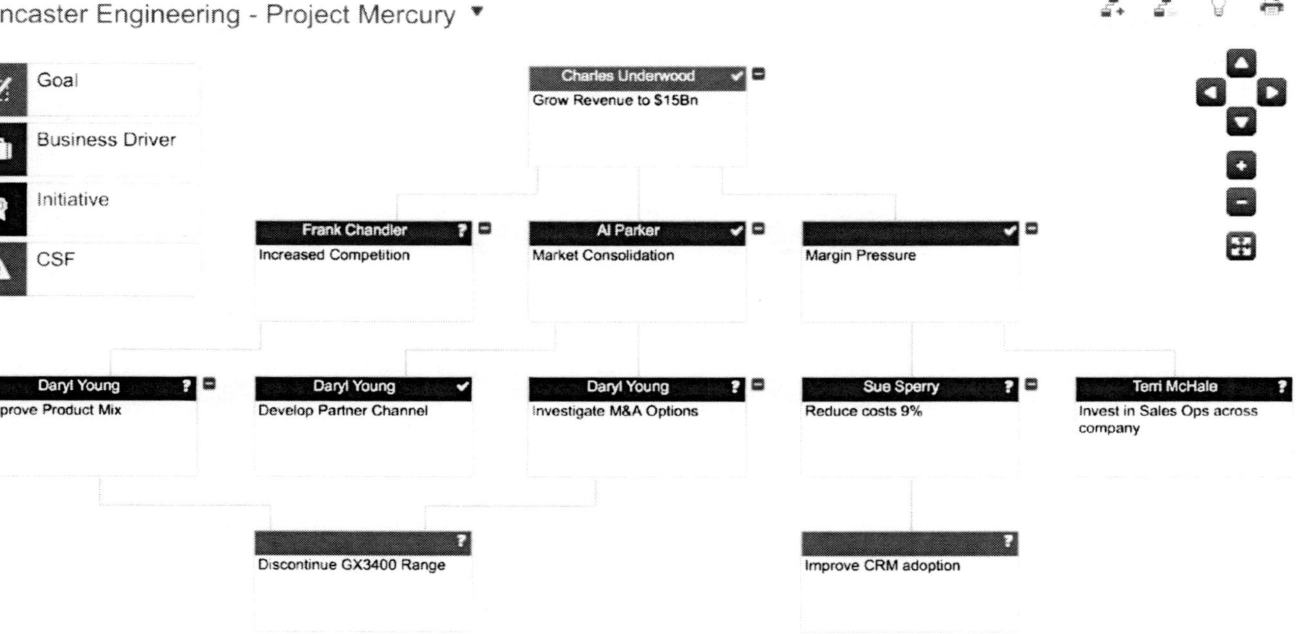

Reduce Risks through Integration

Earlier in this chapter I asked you to think about your largest customer and the most important opportunity that you are working on with them today. I think you will agree that losing an opportunity in a large customer is a big problem. In most cases, when salespeople lose a deal it is not because of product price or features. When the loss occurs in pursuit of new customer, either the opportunity was not well qualified as a deal you could compete for and win, or you were outsold. It is as simple as that. I know: I've been there, and I've tried to come up with other reasons – but either I shouldn't have been in the deal at all – or I was outsold. Sometimes the truth hurts.

Usually when a sales person loses a deal in an existing account, or even worse, loses the whole account, it is because the customer felt that they were underserved or that the sales person did not understand their business.

In either case (new or existing customer), one of your competitors has done a better job of convincing the customer that his solution is a better fit for the customer's requirements, or he has swayed the customer's requirements away from your value; or the customer has not been convinced of the return on investment you offer or has decided not to give you the business because he is not comfortable with you, your product or your company. There is always a reason, and you need to know what it might be, before it happens – particularly in your most important Accounts.

That's where it is important to leverage all of the resources you have in an integrated manner – so that every player on your team knows the role they have to play in a carefully choreographed production. The customer is constantly connected, moving more quickly than ever before – and you need to ensure that your Account Planning activities are systematized and revolve around a hub to which all of your contributors are connected.

Remember what I said earlier. When things move at the velocity described at the beginning of this chapter, and where business customers have been conditioned to act like impatient consumers, bad things happen if you have not put a communication, collaboration, and response system in place that meets their expectations.

Once you do, you can move quickly – and gain ground. In today's fast moving world – velocity matters.

CHAPTER 6

SEGMENT FOR PRIORITY

As a sales professional, one of the few things you can control is your selling time. This is your most precious time – when you're not reporting, managing, or attending company meetings – and you don't want to waste it. You need to know what to prioritize and where to spend that valuable time. To make that determination, you must have a clear picture of the possible options.

The first step on this journey, in the context of Account Planning, is understanding the structure of your Account. This is the purpose of Account Segmentation, the process of identifying and prioritizing all of the discrete divisions or Business and Service Units within an enterprise account – where you might uncover problems that the customer is trying to solve where there may be a fit for one of the solutions you offer. Consider it market research and planning – you're building a map of the Account, and you are beginning to change the way you sell.

Earlier, I wrote that, in order to change the way you sell, you need to change the way that you view your Accounts. You need to view your Account as a marketplace.

Figure 15: The Marketplace – Segmented

This means that you need to understand that market, and then begin segmenting it into a number of sub-segments with two goals in mind:

- Cover as many segments as possible where the return justifies the effort, and
- Penetrate each segment as deeply as possible.

In an ideal world you would like to cover 100% of the market. Realistically, because resources are scarce and your time is at a premium, you have to make choices about which segments to cover, how you cover them, and how much energy and resources you expend on each segment. This means that you must prioritize your efforts in areas that will generate the most opportunity, allowing you to utilize your resources most effectively, and providing a foundation for you to grow in the account.

You must select those areas in the Account that are *Important to Customer* and *Important to You*. This market view of the Account will allow you to prioritize both *where* you sell and *what* you sell.

Let's use the Segmentation Map in Dealmaker Smart Account Manager (**Figure 16**) as an example of how you might visualize the relative attractiveness of each Business and Service Unit.

Business Units and Service Units

In his book *Competition in Global Industries,* Michael Porter said that there are essentially two kinds of entities in any corporation. First there are Business Units, which manage the primary activity or the customer-facing activity of the company. Second there are Service Units, which service or support the Business Units. From earlier discussions you know the difference between the two.

Identifying and understanding your customer's Business Units allows you to begin to understand the customer's planning and investment processes. Their focus and behavior is probably more similar to yours than to their colleagues in the Service Units. Typically, like you, Business Units are chasing revenue and their reason for being is to be successful in their chosen (external) marketplace. For this reason they typically also have well-identified competitors.

In contrast, the market that a Service Unit serves is internal to the enterprise: the business unit – or often more than one. Service units may be centralized in one location, distributed throughout the enterprise (aligned with Business Units) or both. Service Units can be – and are – outsourced. Good examples are payroll, IT support desks, and order fulfillment.

They take it to heart when Bob Dylan says "You gotta serve somebody."

 *You gotta serve somebody.*

Gotta Serve Somebody, Slow Train Coming, Bob Dylan, 1979

To internalize these concepts for yourself you could select one of the Large Accounts you are working on and seek to identify the Business Units and Service Units in the Account.

Segmenting your Account

When there are multiple discrete target areas in an Account you must treat it as a marketplace. Thinking of it this way gives you a framework to think strategically about where in the marketplace to apply resources. Are there market segments that are more attractive than others? Are there some that you should avoid? How do you know?

By taking this approach, Account Planning can help you to maximize the return you get from an existing or new strategic Account, and you can use this element of the Account Planning methodology as your compass as you navigate your marketplace.

Segmenting an Account into its constituent Business Units helps you to draw the Segmentation Map (**Figure 16**), the visualization or mapping of the intersections between the Account or Plan units in your Account Plan – the *where* you are selling – with the solutions that you can provide – the *what* you are selling.

Figure 16: The Segmentation Map

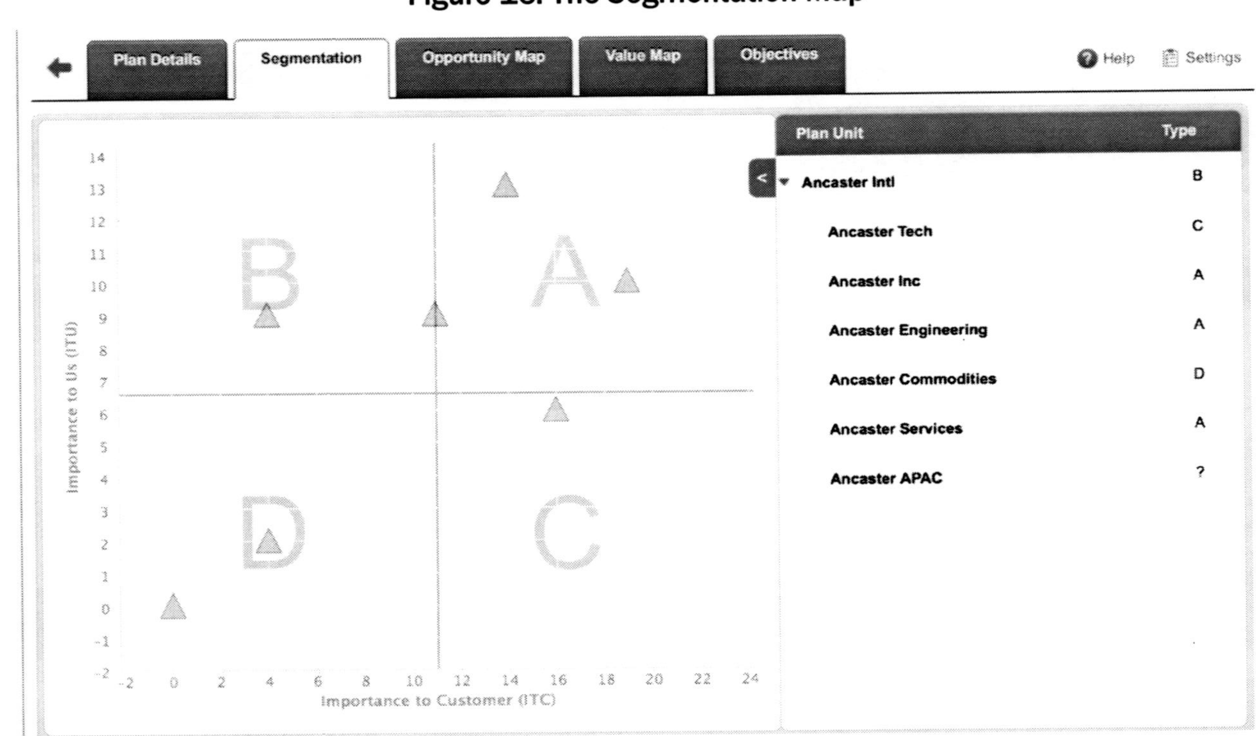

Before you do that everyone on the Account Team needs to understand the context. Remember that good Account Management is generally not a solo sport. While it is the role of the Account Manager to set and communicate the strategy for the Account, each team member should play his or her part in building the picture of the Account and all need to be following the same guidelines to know where you should prioritize your resource allocation.

Figure 17: The Segmentation Map – Value

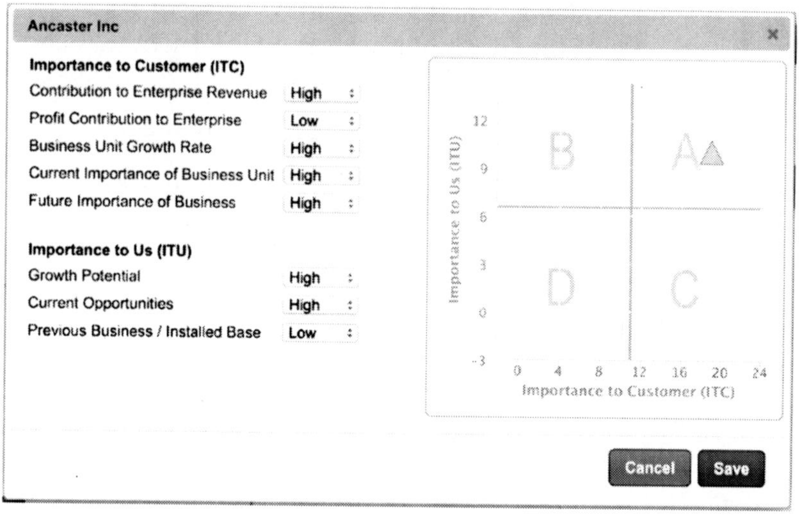

Ancaster Inc

Importance to Customer (ITC)

Contribution to Enterprise Revenue	High
Profit Contribution to Enterprise	Low
Business Unit Growth Rate	High
Current Importance of Business Unit	High
Future Importance of Business	High

Importance to Us (ITU)

Growth Potential	High
Current Opportunities	High
Previous Business / Installed Base	Low

Importance to Us (ITU)
12 9 6 3 0 -3
B A
D C
0 4 8 12 16 20 24
Importance to Customer (ITC)

Cancel Save

There are only two axes to consider as you plot success: *Importance to the Customer* (horizontal) and *Importance to You* (vertical). When you can get these two sometimes-opposing forces to align, really good things happen.

Importance to the Customer can be measured by:

- **Revenue Contribution to Enterprise**: A key ingredient in determining the importance of the business unit. However, high revenue generation alone does not make the business unit important.

- **Profit Contribution to Enterprise**: The unit may generate high revenues, but if it also has high overhead, the profit contribution will be small.
- **Unit Growth Rate**: Growth rate is also a factor to consider when looking at importance. If the unit has 'flat' growth or is in a mature market, then it may not be strategic to the customer. Alternatively, if the unit is small but has triple digit growth trends, then it may be more important than its current revenue suggests.
- **Current Importance of Unit**: How important is the business unit in terms of the enterprise's current goals and direction?
- **Future Importance of Unit**: How important is the business unit in the enterprise's future goals and direction? Is the customer basing their enterprise strategy around this unit?

In order to determine the importance of the Business Unit to the customer, you must look at it from several different angles. Keep in mind that, as you use the Segmentation Map to select your key Business Units, you are trying to focus on those units that are most important both to the customer and to you. All the units have some level of importance either to you or to the customer, but again since you can't focus on them all, you need to focus on those that are of the most importance. So, you are looking at the relative importance of the Business Unit.

Importance to Us is the other axis you need to consider. Account Planning is not entirely altruistic. At the end of the day you are looking to make progress for your business and you need to determine how each unit maps against the considerations that you care about. These should include:

- **Growth Potential:** First, consider the unit's growth potential – your ability to initiate and develop new opportunities within the Business Unit based on the 'fit' of your products and services and the customer's requirements.
- **Number of Current Opportunities:** Consider the number of Current Opportunities you have in the specific unit – projects that you identified as already in your sales pipeline.
- **Previous Business / Installed Base:** Another criterion you want to consider is the amount of business you have done with the customer in the past. What products and services is the customer already using? Some of them may be in maintenance mode – or maybe there are other recurring revenue or up-sell opportunities.

The net result of your efforts, looking at things from two different angles, considering both perspectives – the customer's interests, as well as what is important to you – is the Segmentation Map – your chart to success.

Selecting the Right Business Units

Now that you've had the opportunity to evaluate and plot each Business Unit on the Segmentation Map, let's talk about how you decide which units to include in your Account Plan.

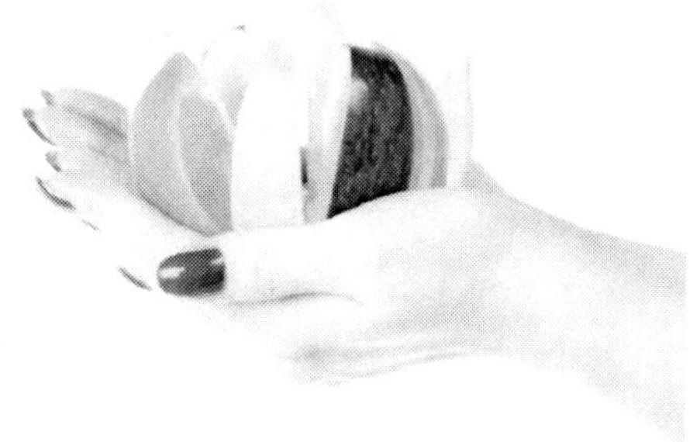

You've got to pick the right segments, and make sure you avoid the lemons.

The Segmentation Map in **Figure 16** shows four quadrants:

- **A Quadrant:** The upper right quadrant contains the Business Units of the highest mutual importance to the customer and to you. They are the main units you want to use to build your Account Plan.
- **B Quadrant:** The upper left quadrant contains Business Units of low or undefined importance to the customer and high importance to you. Although these units may represent a good source of revenue for you, your customer may feel that they are not getting the return on investment they expected from them. After consideration, you may want to include some of these units in your Account Plan.
- **C Quadrant:** This quadrant contains the Business Units of high strategic importance to the customer but undefined or low importance to you. These units typically constitute Potential Opportunities. However, you need to investigate their value to you. If selecting these units for your Account Plan, consider the investment you need to make in resources and time.
- **D Quadrant:** The lower left quadrant contains Business Units of low strategic importance both to the customer and to you. Remember that you are assessing relative importance. However, you should question their value as part of your plan.

It should be pretty clear that the top right-hand quadrant is where you will find your most obvious targets for sales investment. Here are the areas where your objectives should be aligned with those of your customer. These are the 'A' units and generally you will choose these as the areas to prioritize.

But in order to prioritize what matters, you must de-prioritize the areas that will not meet the necessary threshold. It becomes pretty clear from the Segmentation Map that the 'D' units (those in the bottom left-hand quadrant) should be dismissed from future consideration for direct coverage.

The Account Team should mull over the other two quadrants – the 'B' units and the 'C' units – very carefully. The only way that you can determine that a unit belongs in the top right is through an appreciation of value – and that requires education, discussion, and exploration.

Prioritizing by de-prioritizing allows you to apply your valuable resource – selling time – where it's needed most. Maintaining a watching brief on these two secondary quadrants means you're less likely to miss opportunities – and you get to keep an eye over any approaches from the competition.

Relentless and resourceful research will inform your Account Segmentation, helping you to think like your customer. As you take your virtual place at the customer's boardroom table, empathizing with their risks and challenges, fears and aspirations, you will be prompted to zone in on those account units where your solution aligns with the customer's strategic imperatives. Decisions that you make here build the foundation of your Account Plan, so it is worth taking the time to make your determinations carefully. Segmentation helps you to make intelligent decisions so that you do not over- or under-invest in a specific Business Unit.

Now you're on your way. The course is charted for you. *You know where to sell.* Remember, if you use the customer's perspective as your navigational aid, you're more likely to stay afloat.

CHAPTER 7

PEOPLE AND PROBLEMS

In June 2012, Angela Ahrendts, CEO of Burberry appeared on the cover of *Fortune* magazine. As the magazine reported it:

> Last May, Burberry CEO Angela Ahrendts flew to California from her London headquarters to introduce herself to an executive she thought could be critical to the future of her business: Salesforce.com CEO Marc Benioff.
>
> When the two met at the Ritz-Carlton in Half Moon Bay, they stood in the hall batting around ideas for 15 minutes before even sitting down. Ahrendts explained her vision: to create a company where anyone who wanted to touch the brand could have access to it.
>
> She just needed a digital platform to make it happen.
>
> Benioff sketched a diagram of how Burberry could become a 'social enterprise,' overlaying technology like Salesforce, SAP, Twitter, and Facebook atop the entire company. (Benioff signed the drawing "Angela + Marc = LIKE," and Ahrendts keeps the framed original – **Figure 18** – in her office.)
>
> "I told him, 'I think I finally met someone who talks faster and has more energy than I do,'" she says. "We just connected."

Figure 18: Marc Benioff's Sketch for Angela Ahrendts

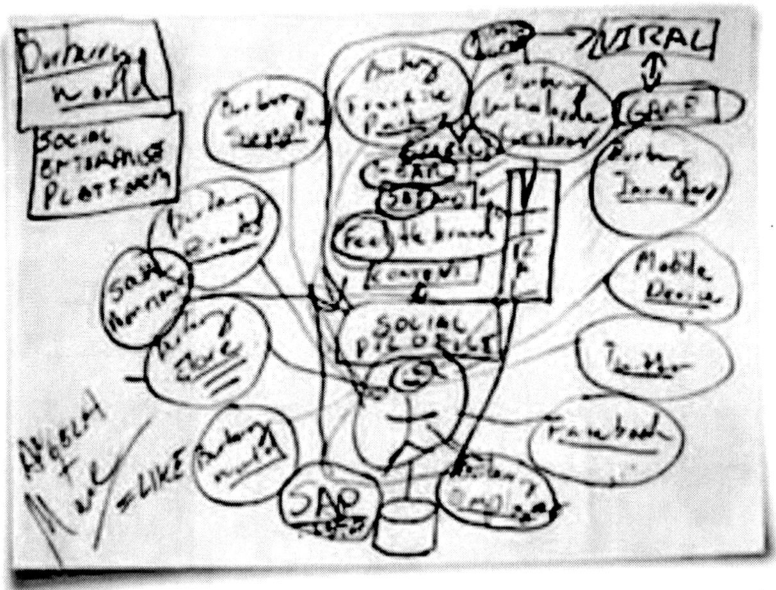

But this is not new for Marc Benioff or salesforce.com. Understanding and recognizing customers has been part of salesforce.com's mantra since the early years.

The following is an excerpt from a press release issued by salesforce.com in 2005:

> **Salesforce.com Announces CRM Success Heroes Award Winners at Dreamforce '05**
>
> New Heroes program spotlights salesforce.com customers whose extraordinary success has made them heroes in the workplace
>
> SAN FRANCISCO, CA – September 13, 2005 – Salesforce.com [NYSE: CRM], the technology and market leader in on-demand customer relationship management (CRM) announced its first class of CRM Success Heroes at Dreamforce '05. Salesforce.com is recognizing customers whose innovative and successful

> implementations of the company's on-demand technology have made them heroes to the people with whom they work.
>
> "'You've made me a hero!' is a common refrain from customers I speak with," said salesforce.com chairman and CEO Marc Benioff. "Our technologies have allowed companies to redefine CRM, and the innovation we are seeing here at Dreamforce is truly inspiring. So we decided to share these incredible success stories with the larger community."

And here is an excerpt from a press release issued by a customer:

> **Two Esker Executives Named Salesforce.com "Heroes"**
>
> Esker Software VP of Americas Sales Michael J. Wenzel and Director of IT Nicolas Bragard awarded accolades for innovation from CRM leader
>
> DREAMFORCE '05, SAN FRANCISCO, CA – September 13, 2005 – Two executives from Esker Software, the leading provider of automated document delivery solutions and services, were honored today as "Customer Heroes" by salesforce.com at the CRM leader's annual user and developer conference.
>
> Salesforce.com recognized Esker vice president for Americas sales, Mike Wenzel and its director of IT Nicolas Bragard, for their innovative use of the salesforce.com offering and contribution to development of best practices for customer relationship management.

If you Google "salesforce.com hero" you will see that the *customer hero program* (my phrase) goes deep and wide at salesforce.com. Benioff knows how to make his high-profile customers feel special. But more importantly, he, and many of his cohorts at salesforce.com, know better than most how to get underneath the business issues that are uppermost in the customer's mind.

The Burberry / salesforce.com story is a great example of how a supplier took the time to create value for his customer by taking the customer's perspective. In this case, salesforce.com is viewed as a co-traveler on Burberry's journey, the apogee of the supplier / customer relationship.

(I really wanted to use the lyrics from Razorlight's *Burberry Girl* here, but if you know the song, you will understand why I decided it might not be the best thing to do.)

If you have followed the principles outlined in the previous two chapters (**CHAPTER 4: RESEARCH FOR INSIGHT** and **CHAPTER 6: SEGMENT FOR PRIORITY**), you will have arrived at a place where you can take out Dealmaker, your own virtual napkin, and sketch your joint vision with the customer as you develop your account plan.

It is surprising to many people that customers are willing to work with you this way – but being a customer isn't as easy as you might think. Later in this chapter I will show what an automated and integrated napkin might look like as your build out a Strategy Map for your customer. Let's first spend some time considering *why* the customer wants you to do that for her.

Being a Customer is Hard

You'd be forgiven for thinking that being a customer is easier than being a sales person. All the customer's got to do is pick a supplier, right? But when the customer makes that buying decision, we now know that the risk shifts from the supplier to the customer, and the impact on the customer of a poor buying decision is usually greater than the impact on the salesperson of a lost sale. I have said this before, but I think it is important enough to say again:

> The impact on the customer of a poor buying decision is usually greater that the impact on the salesperson of a lost sale.

For a customer to be comfortable, she must be really sure that the supplier has a deep comprehension of her (sometimes unstated) needs. Uncovering or understanding even one's own wants or desires can be an unyielding search. When that quest is filtered through the lens of another, vision is often blurred, and the picture that emerges is uncertain. In a corporate context, personal and company motives sometimes collide, or at least bring with them varying nuances of aspiration, and a panoply of potential wants and needs explodes. Customers and suppliers, sometimes unknowingly, share the consequent anxiety when they meet in the un-choreographed buy-sell dance.

Psychometric studies show that each of us has different approaches to social interaction, leadership, teamwork, and relative strengths or weaknesses when it comes to strategic or tactical bias, detail or big picture orientation, and introspection or engagement. Consider then that, over the course of your business life, you're likely to encounter the full spectrum of customers or buyers who will exhibit varying proclivities for action, engagement, or precision.

Each customer will be different. Some will want to lead the buy-sell interaction; others are prepared to follow the direction of a trusted supplier. More are at their most comfortable when working in collaboration with their supplier – and it's this last category that is most common, and certainly most productive, for both buyer and seller alike.

So, what's the best model for customer interaction? Unfortunately there is no one answer that works in all cases, but there is a proven method that we would recommend that you follow. A collaborative approach to fully describing the problem being addressed is always instructive, even when customers exhibit tendencies of leader or follower.

The Customer's Challenge

Let's spend a little time thinking about a customer who is seeking to work with an external supplier to help her solve her business problem. This example relates to a relatively simple purchase that the customer wants to make. The challenges that are manifest here are quite commonplace – but are dramatically magnified when a customer is looking for a partner to help in developing her business, as is the case when you are working to build an Account Plan with her.

> Carol is a Senior Vice President with a mid-size technology company that we will refer to as TechCo. She has a global role at TechCo, and having been with the company for many years, her portfolio of functional responsibilities has grown in line with her impressive capabilities. At heart though she considers herself a sales person, having started with TechCo as a regional sales representative 17 years earlier, and she enjoys her role as head of sales the most.
>
> The way Carol tells it, she thought her request was fairly straightforward.
>
> > "I just wanted more leads. We were struggling with our numbers. The team wasn't getting up to bat often enough. Marketing just wasn't delivering. So I just went to the market looking for a partner who could get me more leads."
>
> Since Carol's marketing team was upset that it wasn't given the job of solving the problem, she ended up with an inbox full of potential suppliers. She got responses from

the list brokers. Proposals came in from companies who set up appointments for sales people. Email marketing companies, SEO consultants, and social media evangelists came out of the woodwork.

While Carol was sitting at her desk early one morning, her phone rang. Normally Carol's assistant Kathy would have answered the phone and screened the call. This time however, Kathy hadn't yet arrived in the office, and Carol was expecting a call from her head of UK sales, so she answered the phone, and was surprised to find herself engaged in a challenging business conversation about her need for more sales leads.

On the other end of the phone, Martin, the CEO of a boutique marketing consulting company, suggested to Carol that perhaps she should consider that more leads might not be the answer to her problem. He asked her to consider that the problem she really wanted to address started with the fact that the team was struggling to achieve its revenue goals, and that in fact 'getting up to bat more often' might not be the answer. As the conversation unfolded, Carol realized that if she was to get the best from an external supplier she first had some considerable work to do.

Carol brought together some of her top performing sales people and the marketing people to get a better understanding of the internal issues they were really trying to resolve. She needed to understand the difference between the symptom of the problem, its underlying cause, and the consequence of not solving the problem. In short, her first task was to **map out the internal issues**, and she needed a way to achieve that.

As the team began to work together, it became clear to Carol that only a TechCo insider would understand the language they were using. It was specific to the company, and assumed a level of contextual knowledge that she could reasonably expect her team to have, but it was unreasonable to expect an external supplier to speak the same language. She needed a **mechanism to explain the business challenges to a supplier.**

But even if TechCo succeeded in mapping out the internal issues and found a mechanism to explain them to an external party, Carol struggled with how she might **overcome the uncertainty about whether the supplier understood the specific problem** she was trying to solve – now that she accepted that it wasn't really just about 'getting up to bat more often.'

After much effort and guidance from Martin, Carol began to better understand the importance of clear communication between TechCo and any potential supplier. She still struggled with how the value of her efforts might be sustained and wondered how anyone could fully gain alignment between customer and supplier. She wanted to avoid any current or future misunderstanding.

Carol's experience isn't unusual. While sales people worry about what they need to do to win a sale, they often forget that the customer may well be struggling with how to best interact with a supplier. When a customer is buying any non-commodity item, it is always worth taking into account the tasks that the conscientious buyer needs to undertake to maximize the value of the interaction.

We can learn from Carol's story.

The challenge often faced by a customer when looking to leverage the expertise of an external supplier can be summarized as:

1. No easy or established way for the customer to map out the internal customer issues.

2. No mechanism to explain the business challenges to a supplier.
3. Uncertainty about whether the supplier understands the specific problem.
4. Need to gain alignment between customer and supplier to avoid any current or future misunderstanding.

Sometimes the customer has not had the opportunity, or mechanisms, to fully contemplate all of the subtleties of their stated needs. Instead of being frustrated by the apparent lack of progress, it is worth attempting to discern whether part of the problem is the customer's inability to overcome these obstacles, or whether you need to mine further for the truth to get a precise picture of where Mutual Value lies.

Clearly, if the example I outlined above is magnified at an Account level, as opposed to just for an individual opportunity, your chance of progress in the Account is greatly retarded. I would like to outline a process that you might follow to help remove that possibility.

In **CHAPTER 6: SEGMENT FOR PRIORITY**, you took your marketplace — the Account — and divided it into those units that are most important to the customer and to you. Now, to help you better understand your customer as a marketplace, let's begin analyzing those units.

The first step in analyzing your Account as a marketplace is to understand the drivers that impact that marketplace. You can do this by determining the Business Drivers that affect the units you selected, the Customer Initiatives that have been established to address them, and the Critical Success Factors that determine the efficacy of the initiatives.

Figure 19: The Strategy Map (2)

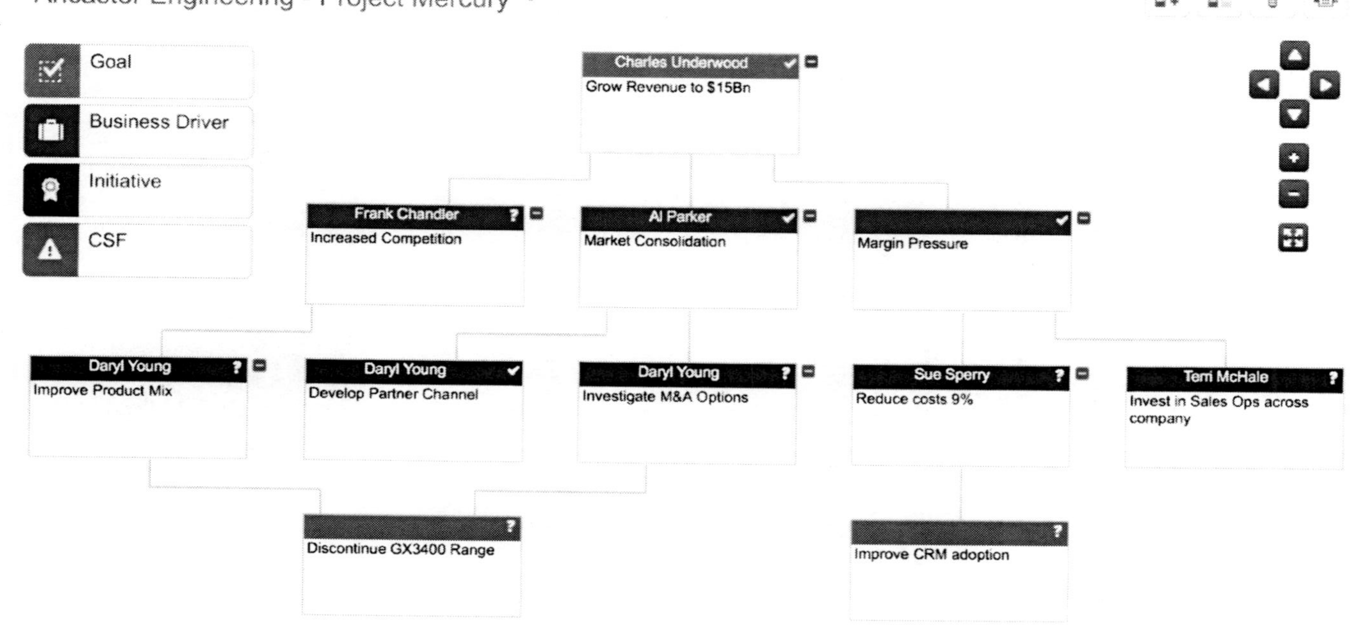

By the time you get to the end of this chapter, you will be able to build a Strategy Map (**Figure 19**) (with your customer), a graphical collaborative framework that assists you and the customer to conceptualize their problem or opportunities areas – in the context of their goals.

Then you can work together with the customer to sketch out how your solutions might be applied to provide the answer. This collaborative approach removes a lot of the frustration that is usually attendant in supplier/customer relationships.

In **CHAPTER 9: FOCUS FOR IMPACT**, I will show you how focusing on your customer's drivers and initiatives can help you to identify new business development opportunities.

Level of Relationship

A better understanding of your customer's business can improve your level of relationship and assist you in entering the customer's decision process earlier. Often, at the start of your relationship, you may find yourself at the bottom of the pyramid—the Vendor level.

Figure 20: The Business Relationship Pyramid

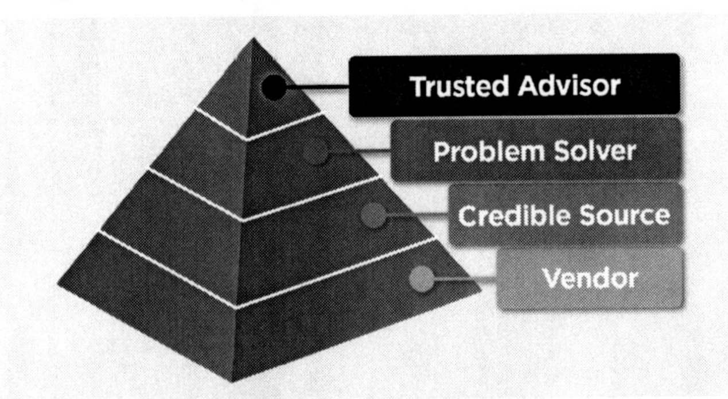

Changing the way you view your account can help you to improve your relationship with the customer. If you view your Account as a market, you can begin to see the drivers that move and shape the units within it. Once you identify those drivers you can add more value by addressing the customer's specific needs. Better understanding and identification of your customer's needs directly correlates to improving your relationship with the customer.

Take a look again at the Business Relationship Pyramid in **Figure 20**. I'd like you to think about your current relationship with your customer. What level are you at today? Keep in mind that your level of relationship can vary from unit to unit.

The Business Relationship Pyramid shows four levels:

- **Vendor:** At the Vendor level, your relationship is based solely on your product and your company's ability to deliver. Generally you become aware that your customer has a specific need only when you receive an RFP. So, you are reactive in responding to the customer's needs.
- **Credible Source:** As a Credible Source, you consistently meet or exceed the customer's expectations. Your contact or coverage in the account is with lower level managers across multiple functions.
- **Problem Solver:** As a Problem Solver, your relationship with the customer is more proactive. You may help the customer generate the RFP. You are aware of existing problems and develop solutions for them. You also have contact with the customer at higher management levels within multiple functions and across multiple units.

- **Trusted Advisor:** At the Trusted Advisor level, you and the customer explore emerging needs and new directions on a confidential basis. Therefore, your role in the customer's organization is similar to that of a consultant. Your contacts within the company are at the executive level throughout the enterprise.

In order to improve your relationship with the customer, you first have to understand where you're starting from – in the context of the customer's decision cycle. Typically, when a customer is making an investment, they are doing so in response to a problem they have to solve, or an opportunity that they can see.

Figure 21: The Customer's Decision Cycle

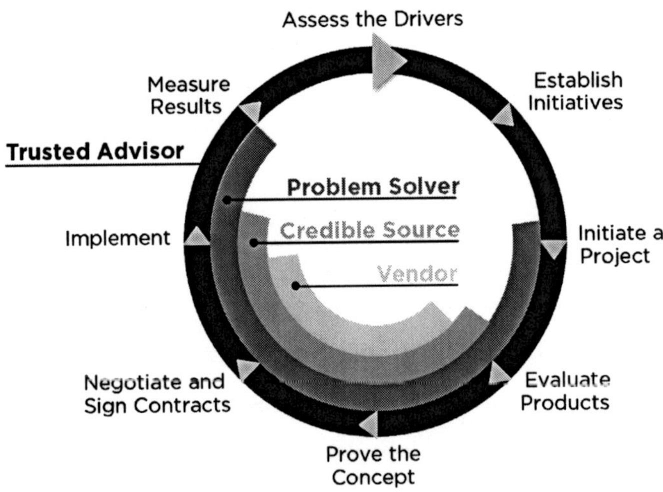

Business Needs drive the customer's decision process. Ideally you are helping them shape their Business Needs and crafting an initiative with them to meet their requirements. Whether you are involved or not, the decision cycle will follow a similar pattern, and understanding that cycle will inform your activities.

Once the problem or opportunity is understood, objectives and requirements are determined. In the past the customer might move straight to the RFP (Request for Proposal) stage. In today's Internet-centric world, customers may look to online sources, social networks, or peer recommendations to further inform their next steps. At some point, suppliers are invited to provide information in the form of an RFP or other mechanism, and the customer evaluates the different offerings. Clearly, the earlier you are involved in the cycle, the better position you are in to shape the requirements, and to influence the progression along the way.

The customer will choose the product or service that meets their requirements and negotiate contracts with the chosen supplier. The chosen product or service is then implemented. Finally, the solution is measured for return on investment (ROI) against metrics established earlier in the process.

As a Product Vendor, you enter the process when the customer is ready to evaluate products. You are generally not involved in measuring the results of your work.

Moving up the relationship pyramid, notice that your role in the customer decision-making process expands. At the Credible Source level, you are now entering the process just before the customer is ready to evaluate products or solutions to address their needs.

As a Problem Solver, your involvement expands further. Now you enter the process just before the customer has initiated a project and you are involved in the measurement of the results.

At the Trusted Advisor level, you really don't ever enter – or exit – the process. Your involvement with the customer is more cyclical. You may recommend areas that the customer should investigate and develop. Or, when the customer has a need, they come to you and together you assess the problem.

What is one advantage that a Trusted Advisor has that allows them to enter the decision process earlier? Knowledge of the customer's needs! Often, before the customer has even identified those needs themselves. Uncovering business needs and requirements, and defining solutions for the customer differentiates you in the Account and permits you to gain a large measure of influence over the decision process. You gain more influence than if you engage early in the process but do not participate in the definition of the business needs for a solution.

What do you suppose happens to the number of competitors when you enter the decision process earlier? Clearly, if you are doing your job well, and helping the customer uncovering their needs, you have a distinct competitive advantage, and the customer often will feel that there is little need to go to the market to look for alternative suppliers. That way the number of competitors is reduced and the pressure on price is correspondingly reduced.

Remember what I said earlier: operating at Trusted Advisor level with your customer is certainly a desirable goal. But, if your customer is not willing to invest with you at this level then you are wasting your resources and potentially endangering your relationship with the customer. Conversely, if your customer does want to work with you at the Trusted Advisor level and you are operating at the Product Vendor level, you are opening yourself up for competitive vulnerability and risk.

Part of your mission as the Account Team is to deliver Mutual Value. To do this you must clearly understand what your customer values and how, based on your available resources, you can deliver upon that value.

Figure 22: Uncovering Customers' Business Problems

The problem however is that (according to the Dealmaker Index study), only 61% of sales reps are good at uncovering customers' business problems. If you are looking for evidence that this is a worthwhile activity, you might reflect on the fact that those who are good at this important undertaking are 28% more likely to achieve quota.

Business Drivers, Business Initiatives and Critical Success Factors

As mentioned earlier, certain external and internal pressures affect every unit you do business with – these are 'Business Drivers.' To help you align with the customer's needs I will outline here some internal and external pressures that may be causing the customer to act. You might consider these in the context of one of your existing Large Accounts:

- **Financial:** Because Business Units are measured by the enterprise as a source of profit or loss, there is always financial pressure on the unit to increase revenue and decrease expenses.

- **Customers:** Customers are a different source of pressure. External customers make demands on the Business Unit in terms of product and service features, functionality, and cost.
- **Competition:** How about competition? Do you know who your customer's competitors are? Competition creates huge pressure on the Business Unit. Do you know what your customer's competitive advantage is in relation to each of their major competitors? Not only should you know their existing competitors, but you also should know who the potential new entrants are as well. What are some examples?
- **Operational:** What are some of the operational pressures affecting the Business Units you selected? Think about everything your customer must do to create their product or service: manufacturing, distribution, technology, etc. What about the people it takes to run the Business Unit?
- **Regulations:** Does regulatory pressure affect the Business Units you selected? Maybe what you are selling has nothing to do with government or environmental regulations, but you need to understand that it's part of the pressure pushing change.
- **Business Partners:** How do you suppose business partners affect the Business Unit? It's true to say that in most markets today, no firm goes to market alone. Every firm goes to market with other companies who complement or complete their products or services. How do your customer's business partners affect the way they do business?

In summary, if you can understand the Business Needs and the Business Drivers that are driving the leaders of the units, then you can enter the decision process earlier. You also can improve your relationship with the customer by building trust, because you have their needs and interests in mind.

In order to ensure their business stays healthy and continues to grow, the customer must do something to address the drivers that pressure them. As a result, the customer will initiate a project or solution that addresses those drivers, though not all drivers will have related initiatives. Just as you are not able to cover every segment of the Account, your customer is not able to address all the drivers that affect their business. Instead, the customer will focus on those Business Initiatives that are the most essential to the health and functioning of the business.

Business Initiatives are the projects, programs, or plans a company implements to address the Business Drivers. Each initiative will have many associated activities. Not all of these activities demand equal attention; some are far more critical than others. You can help your customer to prioritize their initiatives, and guide them to define the attendant Critical Success Factors for each prioritized initiative by building a Business Strategy Map (**Figure 19**) with them.

Critical Success Factors (CSFs) are the things that have to happen or resources that have to be in place to ensure the success of a Business Initiative. Identifying your customer's CSFs is critical to your success as a team because enterprises dedicate large amounts of their resources to them.

Remember, a Business Strategy Map is a graphical collaborative framework that assists you and the customer to conceptualize their problem or opportunities areas – in the context of their Goals. Constructing this map together is a great way to discover how your solutions might provide the answer and that is how you uncover new Potential Opportunities.

When Marc Benioff sat down with Angela Ahrendts of Burberry to paint his vision of the Burberry Social Enterprise, you can be sure that he first learned about Burberry's Goals and Business Drivers. Together the two CEOs worked their way through the associated initiatives and CSFs, in the pursuit of Mutual Value.

Getting underneath the business problems that your customer has is one of the two most important factors that governs your success in a large account. The other factor is getting the right message to the right people. So, who are the right people, the Key Players in the customer's organization who can influence supplier preference, drive decisions and control outcomes? That is a very important question, answered in the next chapter.

CHAPTER 8

ACCESSING KEY PLAYERS

People, people who need people
Are the luckiest people in the world

People, People, Barbra Streisand, 1964

Recorded in December 1963, and released in September 1964, *People* is the twelfth track and title of Barbra Streisand's fourth solo studio album. It was a newly-recorded version of the much-loved hit song from the Broadway musical *Funny Girl,* in which Streisand starred. The album became the first of Streisand's albums to hit #1 on the *Billboard* album chart, spending five weeks in the top spot.

If you take these lyrics to heart, sales people are indeed the luckiest people in the world – because they need people. Alongside a deep understanding of the customer's business problems, as described in **CHAPTER 7: PEOPLE AND PROBLEMS**, getting access to the right people, knowing how to sell to them, or how to build the appropriate relationship, is critical to success in a Large Account.

As I have worked with talented sales professionals around the world, failing to access Key Players, or to influence them effectively, is always one of the most frequent reasons cited for failure in a sales campaign.

How many times have you, or one of your sales team, spent weeks on a sales campaign only to learn that one of the Key Players that you did not connect with had sent the sale in another direction? Well, you're not alone.

Figure 23: Access to Key Players

Only
54%
of reps can
access key
players
And those
reps are
30%
more likely to
achieve quota

According to the Dealmaker Index, just over half of sales reps are effective at accessing Key Players, and of course those who are successful are more successful at achieving quota. They are granted return access, of course, because each time they visit they bring gifts of valuable insight born of continuous research and consideration of the customer's perspective.

But it is not just about accessing people, it is equally important to understand clearly what each individual wants to achieve. Personal motivation is as important as company motivation. When you can tap into the personal dreams or aspirations of the individual and connect on a more intimate level you get to understand what is really important to him. Then your actions can be more effectively directed.

In the words of Annie Lennox of Eurythmics, "everybody is looking for something."

Sweet dreams are made of this ...
Everybody's looking for something.

Sweet Dreams (are made of this), Sweet Dreams, Eurythmics, 1983

The secret however is to recognize that what 'everybody' is looking for might not be what is valued by that one person that you want to influence.

Here is an example.

In 2010, I was quite excited by a new innovation that we had developed at The TAS Group. Leveraging the knowledge captured through all of the millions of sales cycles that we had measured in Dealmaker, and applying its intelligent rules engine, we launched Dealmaker Genius.

Using Dealmaker Genius, any sales professional could create a customized sales process for their own business in about 15 minutes. We decided to provide this service for free. Prior to the availability of Dealmaker Genius, companies either would get by with their own in-house designed sales process, or they would pay a consultant tens of thousands of dollars to design a sales process for them.

Figure 24: Dealmaker Genius

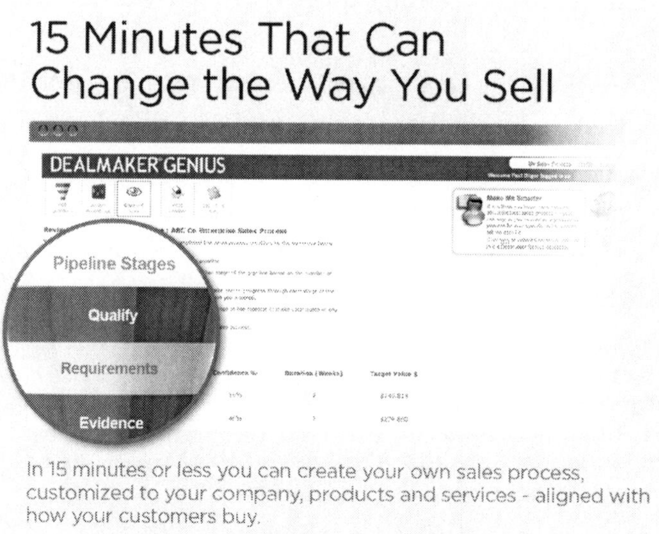

Now they could learn from the experience we had gained from working with the best companies in the world to design their own sales process. We even incorporated crowd-sourcing to continuously improve the Dealmaker Genius knowledge base.

Dave Stein, CEO of ES Research, reviewed Dealmaker Genius, and in a blog post entitled *There Are No Excuses Anymore,* he said:

> For the experienced sales leader, this is better than sliced bread. Rather than spending time and money on tips and tricks with little sustained impact, being able to create a customized sales process for their own business can set them on the path to lasting, measurable sales performance improvement ... I'd be hard-pressed to accept any excuses from process-averse sales leaders as to why they wouldn't avail themselves of this tool and the benefits that it will bring.

Had we found the something that everybody was looking for?

Well, not quite.

The reaction to Dealmaker Genius was so positive, I thought that it might be a good tool for salesforce.com to promote, or to provide for free to its customers. Surely Marc Benioff would be interested!

I was right and wrong at the same time. Here is an extract from our email conversation.

> **From:** Donal Daly
> **Sent:** Sunday, March 07, 2010 6:30 AM
> **To:** Marc Benioff
> **Subject:** Dealmaker Genius - might be of real value to salesforce.com customers
>
> [Personal preliminary content] ...

> I think you will find this interesting – a web 2.0 app that intelligently creates sales processes.
>
> **The TAS Group Releases Dealmaker® Genius, Free Product Enabling Sales Professionals to Create a Customized Sales Process in Minutes, Saving Thousands of Dollars and Weeks of Effort**
>
> *Dealmaker Genius Utilizes Knowledge Base, Domain Expertise and Crowdsourcing to Build the First Free, Global, Intelligent, Online Sales Process Resource* (The press release is attached)
>
> Also, you might enjoy this 3min video that explains how/why we are doing this: http://bit.ly/9f3VSB
>
> Best regards,
>
> Donal

Marc responded by asking me whether I had built Dealmaker Genius natively on Force.com, salesforce.com's development platform. Once I explained the reasons why we had not used Force.com – I was justifying my approach, not really a great idea in hindsight – Marc quickly lost interest.

I had made a rookie error. I assumed that just because lots of people reacted positively to Dealmaker Genius – we've had thousands of users of the free capability at **www.DealmakerGenius.com** – then Marc Benioff would react just the same way as 'everyone' else.

Of course I should have known better. This was right at the time when salesforce.com was accelerating its expansion from being primarily a CRM-only company to the platform company that it is today with the Force.com capability at the center of that journey.

Thankfully, the story didn't end there. Marc was gracious enough to introduce me to George Hu (Chief Operating Officer) and Ron Huddleston (SVP Global ISV and Channel

Alliances) at salesforce.com. I probably should have started the conversation with George and Ron in the first place.

That was the beginning of the current chapter in our partnership with salesforce.com and the start of our journey to deploying the entire Dealmaker sales performance automation solution natively on their Force.com platform. So the effort was not wasted – but it wasn't as effective as it could have been had I been smarter in my approach.

The key message from this story however is that, without adequate focus on what my buyer wanted, and lacking attention to the other attributes of my buyer, and ignoring the fact that there were others who were important to the buying decision, my pursuit was never going to successful.

In this chapter I will discuss how to describe and navigate the customer's organization, uncover who are the right people – the Key Players who can influence supplier preference, drive decisions and control outcomes – and discern what drives them to make decisions. This will allow you to determine the level of relationship that you have and the real consequence of the relationship gap.

Culture and People

There is an old adage that says "Companies don't buy, people buy." The message is that, in order to get a company to buy something from you, you have to get the people in the company to buy. Of course this is true, but I don't subscribe to the notion that the two are disconnected.

A company, its personality, culture, business outlook, market position, business pressures and consequent buying proclivities, are in fact an attribute of the company itself as well as of the people in the company. There is a 'chicken and egg' situation here. Companies have personalities and culture and when someone joins an organization, they are influenced by those attributes; on the other hand a company is made up of people, whose personalities and attributes are themselves influencers on the overall personality of the company. It is not sufficient to consider just one or the other.

One of the biggest mistakes made by many sales professionals is assuming that all customers are created equal. It's as if they expect some alchemist to stir a magic potion and to serve up cookie-cutter customers, each with the same level of technical savvy, common approach to risk, and similar awareness of their need. But, of course, it isn't so.

While it's reasonable to expect that companies of like profile might make parallel purchases of similar products, the particular peculiarities of a buyer in one company may well dictate that he doesn't even know that he has a need – even when his counterpart in another company has successfully completed the implementation and progressed to his next project. Customers are different, and you need to embrace the buyer's perspective. It's his money after all, and doing so will help you get it.

At Bang & Olufsen, designers rule the world: products are not designed based on extensive market research or focus groups – but on the gut-feel of the designers. At UPS, all process is implemented with militaristic precision. At Cirque de Soleil, each theatrical presentation still bears the critical and creative mark of the founder's unique perspective. At Nordstrom, customer service reigns supreme.

When these companies make purchases, do you think the buying processes they adopt are identical? Well, of course not! A company's culture – the combination of practices, behaviors, and values that drive the organization, impacts how the company buys, and therefore how you should determine how you might sell to it.

There are four types of culture you should consider:

- Bureaucratic.
- Entrepreneurial.
- Collaborative.
- Individualistic.

Each requires a different selling approach, so you need to assess the prevalent culture in your target customer to correctly position yourself, your company, and your value proposition. Let's consider how to recognize the culture and how to position accordingly.

When the culture is **bureaucratic**, everything will be very structured, and very controlled. Whoever dictates policies and procedure will be the source of power and that's where you need to focus.

Figure 25: Culture: Bureaucratic

Attributes of a Bureaucratic Culture	
Decision-making	Highly structured, formal
Work Structure	By function in silos
Communication	Controlled and deliberate
Control Mechanism	Policy and procedure
Source of Power	Who dictates policy & procedure?
Recommended Approach	
Pay attention to detail Learn the system Look for help to navigate the system Use formal written communication Follow the chain of command	

The **entrepreneurial** culture is fast moving, and revolves around the leader. Unless you're aligned with the visionary one, your chances of success are slight.

Figure 26: Culture: Entrepreneurial

Attributes of an Entrepreneurial Culture	
Decision-making	Centralized and fast
Work Structure	New opportunities
Communication	Rapid, externally-oriented
Control Mechanism	Leader's vision, extreme loyalty
Source of Power	Who is connected to the leader?
Recommended Approach	
Act fast Align with the visionary Focus on projects easily connected to the vision Be open and prepared for change	

When the culture is **collaborative** you need to be too. Committees rule. Individuals make very few decisions in isolation. Process is across teams with clear measurements.

You need to respect the customer's team process and align with project initiators.

Figure 27: Culture: Collaborative

Attributes of a Collaborative Culture	
Decision-making	Consensus-driven
Work Structure	Business Unit or Cross-functional
Communication	Open
Control Mechanism	Process / Objectives measurement
Source of Power	Who initiates projects and measures results?

Recommended Approach
Sell to the team Cover all members of the team Focus on common ground Show respect for the team

The **individualistic** culture is hard to sell to because there's little centralized decision-making. It's like an amalgam of multiple fiefdoms.

Each needs to be sold to separately. Cross-unit references might help – but not always.

Figure 28: Culture: Individualistic

Attributes of an Individualistic Culture	
Decision-making	Decentralized
Work Structure	Projects and expertise
Communication	Only when essential
Control Mechanism	Individual self interest
Source of Power	Who can perform? Who has expertise?
Recommended Approach	
Focus on the top performers Be prepared to build many relationships Respect their time Don't expect conformity Bridge communication gaps	

Understanding your customer's culture is key to helping you recognize how decisions are made.

I definitely thought that I had a really good understanding of salesforce.com's culture, and I probably did. But I just did not apply it to my approach. Marc Benioff is nothing if not entrepreneurial, and that culture pervades the whole company.

If I look at the approach I should have taken, and followed my own advice (based on the table above), I should have known to:

1. Act fast.
2. Align with the visionary.
3. Focus on projects easily connected to the vision.
4. Be open and prepared for change.

I clearly did not deliver on points 2 and 3, and therefore I was less effective than I might have been.

Culture is a bit like an iceberg. What you can't see is often greater than what you can. Look beyond the obvious to ascertain the culture – then adapt your approach accordingly.

Mapping the Organization

As I've said earlier, most deals are not lost because you don't have the best solution or the best price or the best terms and conditions. They are usually lost because you didn't understand the people or problems. You will remember that the purpose of Account Planning is to:

> Build long-term business relationships in a complex marketplace that enable us to create, develop, pursue, and win business that delivers mutual value.

To build long-term business relationships you need to understand how the organization works, and the politics of the organization as it relates to your goal for that Account. You must be clear on the different dimensions of hierarchy and influence, the difference between organizational structure and political structure.

Think of it like this. If someone is high in the organizational hierarchy, it doesn't always mean that they are also high in influence. Conversely, even though someone does not have a big title, or does not report directly to the C-level in the company, they may still have significant influence over the outcome of a buying decision or the company strategy.

To determine the impact someone has – their Political Status, you have to map Rank – the formal part of the equation – against Influence – the informal part.

Figure 29: The Political Status Map

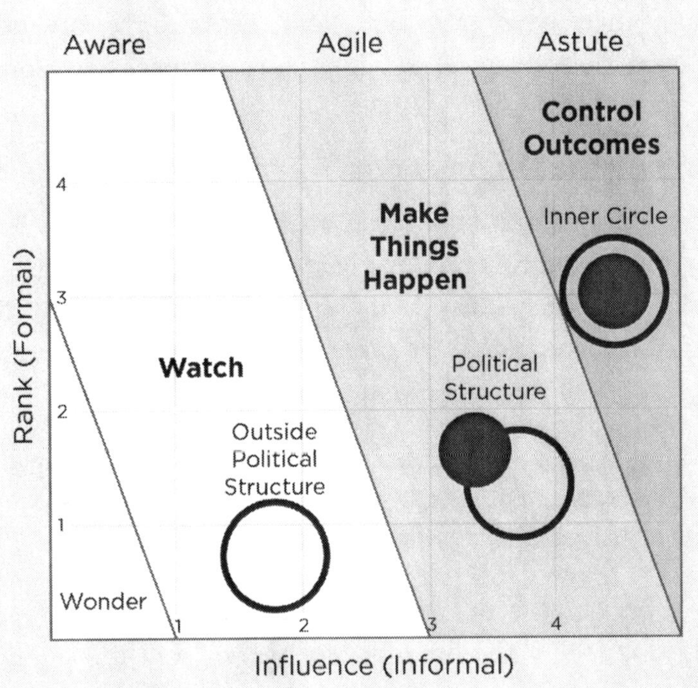

Most people start in a new organization at the bottom left and move up in rank and out in influence. Eventually they cross a threshold: they become aware of the politics of the organization. People to the right of the awareness border can begin to see how the game is played.

When a person learns how to avoid the political traps and become agile enough to dodge the inevitable political conflict, they cross a second border: agility. This is the ability to anticipate events and respond quickly. This is characterized as the *Political Structure* of the organization.

As a person becomes astute at using their rank and influence to build power, they cross another boundary. People to the right of this line not only can respond to events and take advantage of opportunities, but they also understand how to create opportunities. This is the *Inner Circle* of the organization. People in the Inner Circle control what happens within the organization. They have a group of lieutenants in the Political Structure who execute their ideas and make things happen.

Key Players are people in the Inner Circle or in the Political Structure. People outside of the Political Structure – well, they just watch and wonder about what just happened.

You can use the Political Map in Dealmaker to record both your customer's organization structure and political structure. The Political Map provides a visual representation of the people in the buyer's organization who are involved in your opportunity or Account, their relationship to each other and information about each one. You can identify your friends and enemies, and uncover the influencers in the organization.

Conventional wisdom says call high, but this isn't really always good advice for two reasons. Firstly, you need more information than someone's title to determine whether in fact they have influence, and secondly, even those in the Inner Circle are increasingly looking to build consensus in their teams and so they look to those in the Political Structure to guide them.

Measuring Political Status: The following 10 questions will help you to assess the impact an individual might have.

1. Will there be a significant impact if this person says "Yes" or "No" to new initiatives and projects?
2. Is this person responsible for overall Business Strategy for the Business Unit?
3. Do the end-users of your products report to him, or does he represent their interests?
4. Is he the functional leader or the Business Unit leader with profit or loss responsibility?
5. Do people seek out this person's endorsement or expert opinion in areas that pertain to what you sell?
6. Is this person's influence greater than you might expect given his position?
7. Can this person work around the company's policies or procedures to make things happen if he desires?
8. Is his support critical where important initiatives are considered?
9. Does this person sign-off on the financial justification for our project?
10. Will he be measured on the success of your products?

Figure 30: The Political Map

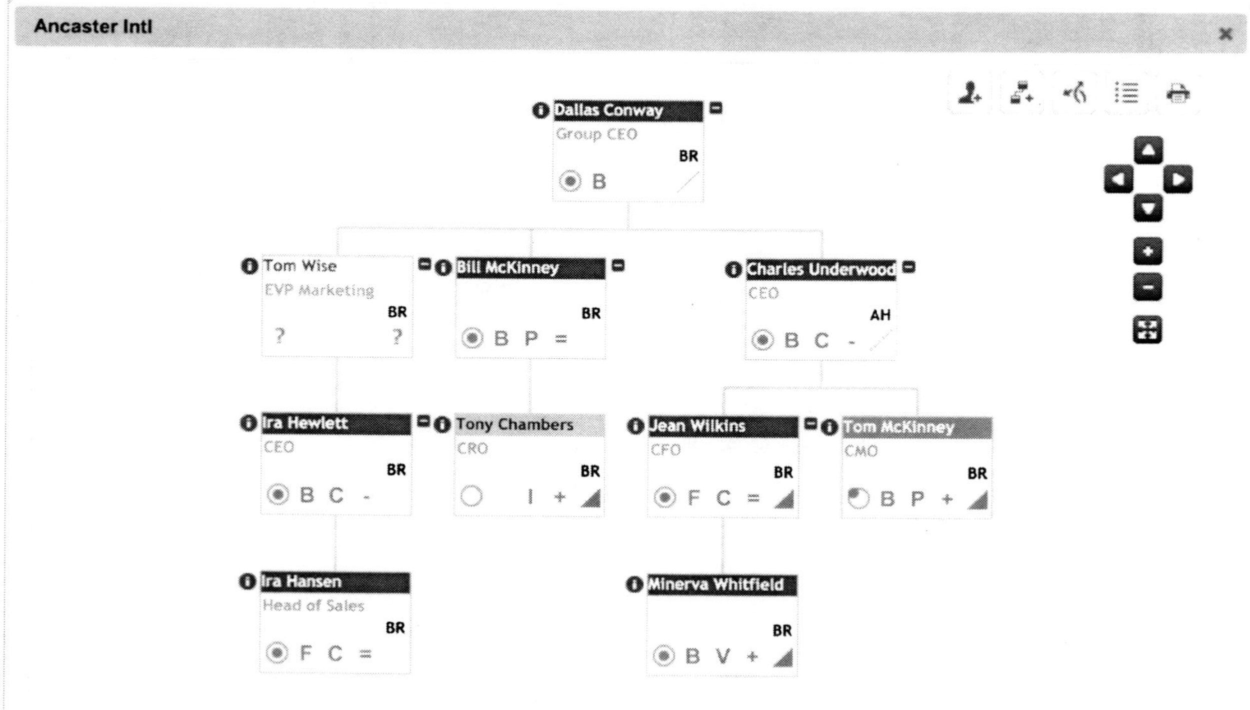

Mapping Personal Attributes

In addition to Political Status, there are a number of other attributes that should guide your actions. These are *Status with Key Players, Decision Orientation* and *Adaptability to Change.*

Status with Key Players: Alongside Influence or Impact, the next critical thing you need to determine for each individual is whether you can count on them to support you as you develop the relationship between your company and theirs. We classify *Status with Key Players* into the five categories listed in the table below.

Figure 31: Categories of Key Players

	Description	Behavior
Mentor	A person who believes that your success is critical to their company or to them personally. A mentor will work to help you win by giving feedback, guidance, political insight, or competitive information. A mentor takes a personal interest in your success and will sell in your absence.	Works with you to develop and test your plan. Shares confidential company information. Actively sells in your absence. Links personal success with your success. Willing to be held accountable for implementing your solution. Openly states that your solution or company is superior.
Supporter	A person who prefers your solution and thinks that you should win. A supporter will typically provide you with information or assistance, if you request. However, they may not be vocal in their support.	Works with you to develop a plan to adopt your solution. Provides you with information about other key players and about the competition's plan. Privately admits your solution or company is superior.

	Description	Behavior
Neutral	A person who shows no preference. They could be ambivalent, or they may have chosen not to display their true feelings. They may not have decided, or you may not have demonstrated sufficient value to gain their open support.	Agrees that your company or solution is a potential fit. Invests time and energy to understand the capabilities of your solution and company. Understands / explains the Compelling Event. Provides information on the key business issues. Thinks a need or problem exists and agrees that a solution or change is desirable.
Non-supporter	A person who believes you shouldn't win and/or prefers an alternative to your solution: your competitor, an internal solution, or nothing at all.	Works with your competitor to develop a plan to adopt their solution. Provides your competitor with information about other key players. Provides your competitor with information about your solution and your plan. Privately admits that your competitor's solution or company is superior.
Enemy	A person who believes that your success will hurt their company or them personally. An enemy will make a special effort to cause you to lose. They may be a mentor or supporter of your competition.	Works with your competitor to develop and test their plan. Shares confidential company information with your competitor. Actively sells your competitor's solution, even in their absence. Links personal success with your competitor's plan. Willing to be held accountable for implementing your competitor's solution. Openly states that your competitor has the best solution.

The following 10 questions will get your brain working to assess the level of support you might expect from an individual and to determine whether they are a friend or an enemy. (You are looking for a lot of *Yes* answers)

1. Does this person talk to others about the value your company can bring to their organization?

2. Has he been a willing reference for you with other customers?
3. Has he introduced / supported you in meetings with other senior influencers in his company?
4. When speaking with others in his company does he refer to you as his chosen business partner?
5. Does he share internal or competitive insights that can help you to strengthen your position?
6. Does he proactively advise you when issues arise in his organization that might affect your position in the Account?
7. Do you consider him a partner that you can count on to help you develop the value proposition for his business area?
8. Does he speak with Key Players about the value that you have brought to his company?
9. Does he look for your input on general issues that are not specifically related to your products?
10. Does he proactively come to you with ideas that might help you win in the Account?

Decision Orientation: The view you see is always dependent on where you are standing; it's the same when someone is making a decision. A customer's decision orientation often is determined by the role they play in a company or their natural affinity to one approach or another. Understanding an individual's orientation is critical to being able to relate to them, and then present solutions to them that align to their needs.

There are four types of decision orientation you should consider:

- Financial.
- Technical.
- Relationship.
- Business.

A **Financial** orientation implies a primary focus on price, cost, and economics. While your product must be viable; numbers and negotiations will be key.

A **Technical** focus is about product functionality and capability. Such individuals are often analytical and detail-oriented. Product demonstrations, benchmarks, and careful deliberation will be key.

Someone with a **Relationship** orientation believes they are forming a business partnership and that you and your company are important to them. While your product must be viable, support, trust, effort, and responsiveness will be important.

A **Business** orientation takes a big picture view and this person can properly balance the technical, financial, and relationship issues. Their vision often extends beyond their company to include their customers, and their competition.

If you want to direct your customer, knowing their inherent orientation bias is essential. That knowledge helps you understand what's important to them and guides how you present value.

Adaptability to Change: How can you anticipate how key players will respond to change? When change is presented, how will they respond? While people do not always respond to change in the same way, they have a certain default approach to change.

Let's discuss some typical categories of a buyer's adaptability to change:

- How would you recognize **Innovators**? They love to be first with the latest ideas. They are attracted to new solutions and products and will experiment with the solution. They are enthusiasts for NEW. But, innovators, while usually influential, rarely have budget. They can also be fickle – looking for instant gratification – and if you don't deliver quickly, they will lose interest and move on to the next shiny object.
- **Visionaries** are revolutionaries. They expect to achieve significant competitive advantage by being among the first. Visionaries are early adopters and often have dollars to buy new solutions or products. However, often they will demand special modifications or improvements to a new solution, tailored to their specific needs.
- **Pragmatists,** sometimes called the 'early majority', believe in evolution not revolution. With a low risk threshold, they adopt products and services with a proven track record of success including references from people they trust.
- **Conservatives** are pessimistic. They tend to question gaining value from investments in new solutions and tend to change only when pressed – when the only alternative is to be left behind. They are typically price-sensitive, skeptical and demanding. Joy!
- **Laggards** are the last to implement new solutions. They generally will do so only when there is no alternative.

Laggards tend to doubt that new solutions or products will provide any value. I'd recommend selling around them if possible.

The ability to categorize each buyer into one of these discrete groups may seem difficult at first but should become obvious as you examine their:

- Track record for implementing new solutions.
- Conversations with you and your team.
- Interactions with your peers.
- Office environment and surroundings.

Figure 32: Buyers' Adaptability to Change

	What they want	What they buy	What to sell
Innovators	State of the art	Trials, tests	Product excellence, innovation
Visionaries	Revolution, recognition	Customized Solution	Future, Competitive Advantage
Pragmatists	Evolution, Solve problems	Total solutions	Proven expertise in solving similar problems
Conservatives	Not to be left behind	Industry standards at low price with no risk	Return on Investment
Laggards	*Status quo*	Enhancements or extensions of existing systems	Investment protection

Figure 32 is a good reference to use to shape the conversation with each of the Key Players in your target account. By

understanding a buyer's adaptability to change, you will know what you should emphasize and where to seek support if your proposition doesn't quite gel.

People Need People

Barbra Streisand advised us at the beginning of this chapter: "People, people who need people, are the luckiest people in the world" – that may or may not be true. What is definitely true is that, without understanding the relationship between people and problems, your progress in an Account will be problematic.

Gaining access to the Key Players is critical. But walking through their doorway will be fruitful only when you have the support of the people around them and when your sense of the personal and company culture is well-developed. Then you can reflect that in how you shape the conversation.

Going back to my interaction with salesforce.com's Marc Benioff regarding Dealmaker Genius, I was fortunate that I got a second chance, and with the support of his broader team, I could execute a strategy fully aligned with their culture and vision. That has led us to the partnership we now have.

When executed well, a strategy that melds people and problems is far more likely to succeed. It will provide you with the ability to uncover and develop many new opportunities – and that is the reason why you are building and managing your Account Plan in the first place.

CHAPTER 9

FOCUS FOR IMPACT

Now we are getting to the fun part. If you've been tracking along with each of the preceding chapters you will know how to research the Account (**CHAPTER 4: RESEARCH FOR INSIGHT**), segment it into its many discrete units (**CHAPTER 6: SEGMENT FOR PRIORITY**), uncover the customer's business problems (**CHAPTER 7: PEOPLE AND PROBLEMS**) and map those to the important people – the Key Players – who make things happen and control outcomes in the business (**CHAPTER 8: ACCESSING KEY PLAYERS**).

One of the most valuable outputs of good Account Planning is an expanded pipeline of opportunities in the account. A deep focus on what the customer cares about, her Business Drivers, Initiatives and Critical Success Factors, will show you the way to find opportunities that your competitors don't see. When you execute this business development activity well, you will have many opportunities to choose from. Then, applying rigorous focus to opportunity selection will deliver maximum impact that will grow your revenue from the account more effectively than any other endeavor.

You will recall that the purpose of Account Planning is to:

> Build long-term business relationships in a complex marketplace that enable us to create, develop, pursue, and win business that delivers mutual value.

You've done the hard work on the marketplace and relationship pieces. Now it is time to focus on the latter part of this sentence:

> .. to create, develop, pursue, and win business that delivers mutual value.

As you know, I like to think about my Account as a marketplace. I use the Opportunity Map in Dealmaker as a graphical representation of that. As you can see in **Figure 33**, this is a useful way to get an overall picture of the opportunities for each of your Solutions mapped to each of the Units in your account.

The Opportunity Map provides a view of the revenue opportunities within your Account Plan. It guides you to map opportunities for your specific Solutions (*what* you are selling) to each of the relevant Plan Units (*where* you are selling). Taking this viewpoint allows you to identify *White Space* – those areas within the Account where the customer has not yet purchased a solution from you – so that you may be able to develop new *Potential Opportunities*.

Whether you use Dealmaker or not, you will need to find a way to record what you are working on and where you might find other opportunities.

Or, to put it another way, it will be helpful to map out your starting position, so that you can see the possibilities before you.

Figure 33: The Opportunity Map (2)

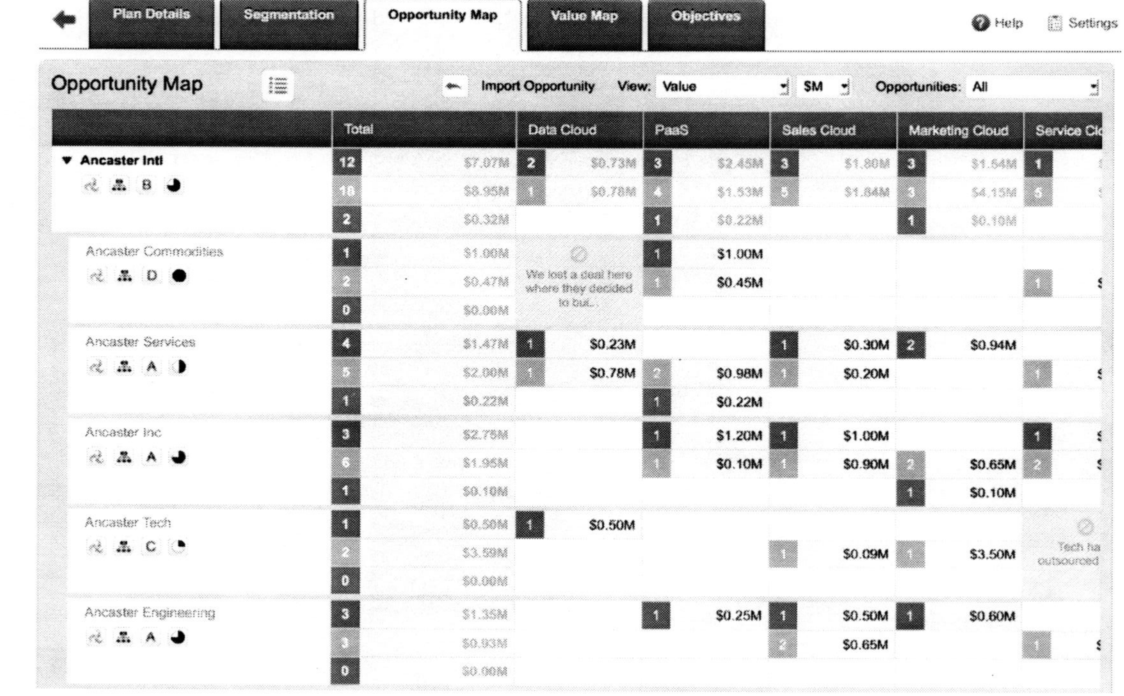

The Opportunity Map: Basic Principles

Let's say there are three different Solutions that you sell in this simple sample Account:

1. Servers for Storage.
2. Printing Services.
3. Security Consulting Services.

There are three Business Units that you have identified:

1. Acme US.
2. Acme EMEA.
3. Acme APAC.

Figure 34: The Opportunity Map – Detail (blank)

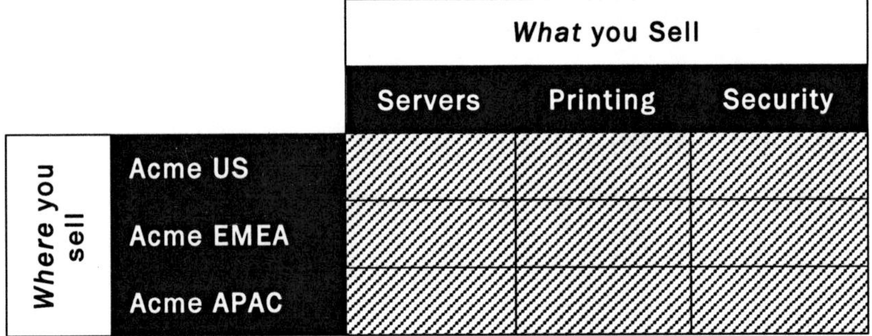

Ideally you want to achieve complete penetration for all of your Solutions into each of the three Units. The hashed area in the graphic above is your marketplace. As you identify opportunities in each of the Units (assuming you have chosen to pursue all of them), you can begin to plot those opportunities on the Opportunity Map.

Figure 35: The Opportunity Map – Detail (revised)

	Servers	Printing	Security
Acme US	$100,000	$80,000	White Space
Acme EMEA	White Space	White Space	$56,000
Acme APAC	$23,000	White Space	White Space

In **Figure 35**, I have added four opportunities to the Opportunity Map, and you can see that there are still five areas where there is White Space. You should explore those areas.

When dealing with a Large Account in the real world, things are a little bit more complicated than this simple view. You rarely start from a blank sheet of paper. There are probably more than three Solutions in your arsenal, and the number of Plan Units in your Account Plan also will likely exceed that number. As you build out the Opportunity Map, it is valuable to record business that has already been won, and deals in which you are currently engaged. That information helps shape the remaining opportunity in the account and makes it easy to identify the White Space.

Different Types of Need and Opportunities

Not all opportunities are created equal – in fact, some are more equal than others. Many sales people, taking just an opportunity focus, will just work on renewing on-going business or trying to close existing opportunities. I refer to these opportunities as *Current Opportunities*. The sales professional or Account Team who separates themselves from the rest, and who plots a way to maximize revenue from the account, explores the total territory within the account to develop new *Potential Opportunities*. Potential Opportunities generally are long-term projects, linked to Business Initiatives, and are, as yet, unqualified.

It is worth taking a few moments to contemplate the factors that shape a customer's awareness of a need. This might guide you to recognize more quickly where Potential Opportunities might exist.

Over the years I have participated in many sales pursuits, interacted with many buyers, and worked with a large number of sales professionals. It is clear that strong patterns exist that correlate the level of awareness that a buyer has of a need to act directly with his propensity to buy something from somebody. That is really no surprise.

However, the parallel pattern is that his level of awareness is inversely proportional to your opportunity to create value. If the buyer does not know that he has a problem or if he cannot identify an opportunity before you point it out to him, you have a strong platform from which you can create value for him.

In my experience there are three types of customer need:

1. Active.
2. Known.
3. Unknown.

Customers who have an Unknown need are a blank canvas and therefore more receptive to value creation, while those in the Active camp are most likely to act soon and will have a higher propensity to buy. Each of these customer types needs to be dealt with differently.

Figure 36: The Propensity to Buy Curve

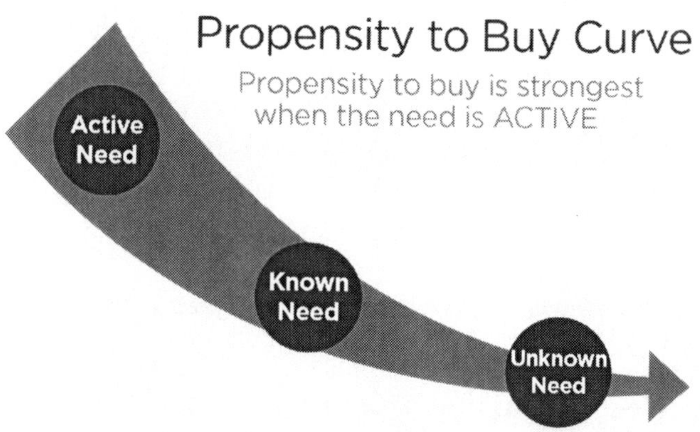

Active Need – Solution Vision: When senior executives move from one organization to another they often will be charged with using the experience gained in their previous company to accelerate the deployment of new systems at their new location. This is just one example of an Active Need. As a buyer, or a prospective customer, this executive will be typical of a customer with an Active Need; he will actively want to work with a supplier to determine quickly the actions to be taken to implement a solution to solve the known problem. He undoubtedly has a vision of the possible solution and understands that it's his responsibility to get the job done.

Without doubt, this is a qualified sales opportunity, and the buying cycle should be shorter than in either of the other two scenarios (Known and Unknown). Hopefully, this is one of your Current Opportunities. However, the bar is set a little higher and it will be somewhat more difficult for you to add value in the application of your product to establish creative solutions, as the customer is already quite proficient, and might well achieve the solution unaided.

You need to focus not just on the 'what', but also on the 'how.' The customer knows what he wants. You need to be able to identify for him how to best apply the product, how you can help better than anyone else, and how you have that insight that will add extra value.

I know what I want, and I know how to get it.

I Know What I Want, Dream Police, Cheap Trick, 1979

Known Need – Unknown Solution: Opportunities abound when a customer knows he has a problem but doesn't know what to do about it. Customers in that situation will place high value on consultative support to aid in the development of a strategic buying vision. They will take comfort from your experience of similar situations with their counterparts in other companies and will value your experience. They will place great value on your ability to identify for them opportunities for applications of your product or service that add value to their business. Going beyond obvious product features, or obvious applications, the customer will want you to help them to uncover business process improvements that you can help them achieve.

Sometimes the customers seem to keep looking forever – like Bono from U2, when he sings "I still haven't found what I'm looking for."

... I still haven't found what I'm looking for.

I Still Haven't Found What I'm Looking For, The Joshua Tree, U2, 1987

Anxiety levels are high and the customer feels at risk because he can't necessarily visualize the solution. If you can transcend the Vendor perspective and be more than 'just a provider,' the customer will go the extra mile for you. He also will be less focused on squeezing your margins, if you join with him in establishing a long-term joint supplier / customer vision.

Figure 37: The Value Creation Curve

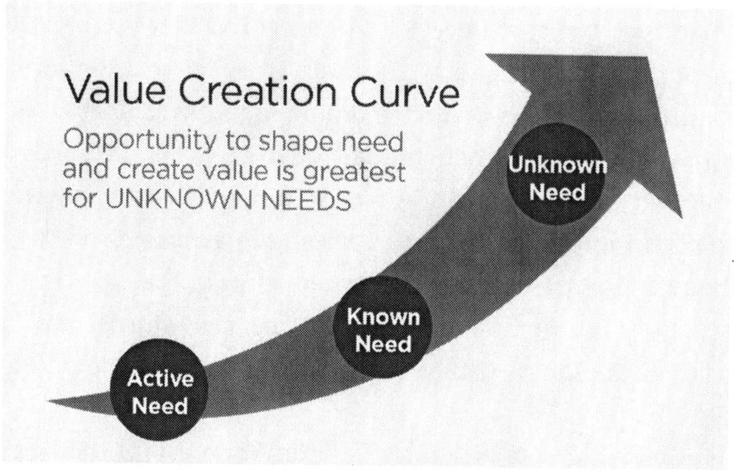

Value Creation Curve

Opportunity to shape need and create value is greatest for UNKNOWN NEEDS

Unknown Need

Known Need

Active Need

Unknown Need – Unknown Problem: Even though your product might be flush with competitive features, each designed meticulously to deliver real business value, the customer might not care, and may not know that there is better way. That's his prerogative! If the customer does not feel business pain, or does not believe that his problem can be solved, or considers that the attendant risks in addressing the problem are too high, then he doesn't see why he should take it on. He can't visualize a reason to change.

Assuming that your product or service offering in fact would deliver quantifiable benefit to this customer, then something is amiss. This is an Unknown Need. The need is there, but the customer has not yet realized it and, from the salesperson's perspective, this is a situation that must be developed by deeply examining the Business Drivers, Initiatives, and Critical Success Factors that are shaping the customer's business decisions, and finding where your solution might be applied to help solve a problem or exploit an opportunity. Here is where you can develop Potential Opportunities.

As of yet, the customer has not accepted that your solution is important to him and will classify it as 'a solution looking for a problem.' He is certainly not engaged in trying to find a solution, because either he is satisfied with the way he currently manages his situation, or just doesn't believe that a viable solution exists. When a customer's awareness of need is unknown, the cost of sale can be very high, the sales cycle is long, and you must place education, 'success stories' and case studies at the top of your agenda as you wait for the penny to drop.

However, no one asked for Twitter, three-point seatbelts or butterflies in an airport.

There was an interesting symmetry in 2011 when Apple announced its native integration of Twitter with iOS5, a new version of the operating system that runs on its mobile devices. At the time there were 200 million iOS devices in use in the world, and 200 million Twitter users. But who would have imagined that 200 million people would ever want to use a service that constrained communication to 140 characters that Twitter enforced. Nobody asked for Twitter. Now 75% of B2B companies in the US use Twitter.

Nobody asked Nils Bohlin at Volvo to invent the three-point seat belt for cars. In the interests of safety, Volvo made the new seat belt design available to other car manufacturers for free. The National Highway Traffic Safety Administration estimates that, in the U.S., the seat belt saves over 4,000 lives and prevents over 100,000 injuries a year.

Nobody asked for butterflies. Yet at Singapore's Chiangi airport you get a real butterfly garden. It is the most applauded and awarded airport in the world.

I'm encouraged by these examples of vision. Sometimes it takes this kind vision to bring Unknown Needs to life.

You will need to determine for yourself how much time it is going to take to develop an opportunity if the need is unknown. Then you must decide whether it is worth pursuing and whether it will be worth winning in the end.

I want you to want me.
I need you to need me.

I Want You to Want Me, In Color, Cheap Trick, 1977

To fully penetrate an Account you need to work not just on the deals that you and the customer know about, or simply extend the deals you have. Instead, you must partner with your customer, and create – not just communicate – value. That's where you find the potential, previously undiscovered, opportunities where you can maximize value for both yourself and your customer.

Let's look again now at the different types of opportunities that together build up a picture of your Opportunity Map.

Current Opportunities are those that are already in the sales cycle, are significant in terms of revenue and / or market value, are either being sourced as brand new opportunities in the account, or are related to up-sell or extension of existing installed solutions.

Up-sell opportunities are important to consider also, since they typically are less competitive and might relate to subscription renewals, long-term service or maintenance contracts, or upgrades or add-ons. There should be an opportunity record already in Salesforce for each Current Opportunity. If not, you will need to create one.

Potential Opportunities usually take longer to develop and close than Current Opportunities. They must be connected to a customer's Business Initiative, and because they are the result of your brainstorming ideas, they may never come to fruition. These are not qualified opportunities, and as such should not be included in your sales pipeline.

> (Note to Sales Managers: You should never treat the Potential Opportunities on an account plan as pipeline or forecast opportunities. If you do, it will discourage your sales team from adding them to the plan, as they will view that practice as only creating hassle for themselves. Also, you will have an inflated view of your pipeline and forecast – and that will surely disappoint.)

In addition to Potential and Current Opportunities there are also some **Won Opportunities,** deals that you successfully close during the lifetime of the Account Plan. Tracking and recording all opportunities on your Opportunity Map helps to give you a fuller picture of your current status so you can clearly see the remaining White Space.

Opportunity Mapping

Let's look again at the Opportunity Map in Dealmaker to see an example of how these opportunities might be represented, and how you highlight where there is White Space for you to explore.

Figure 38: The Opportunity Map (3)

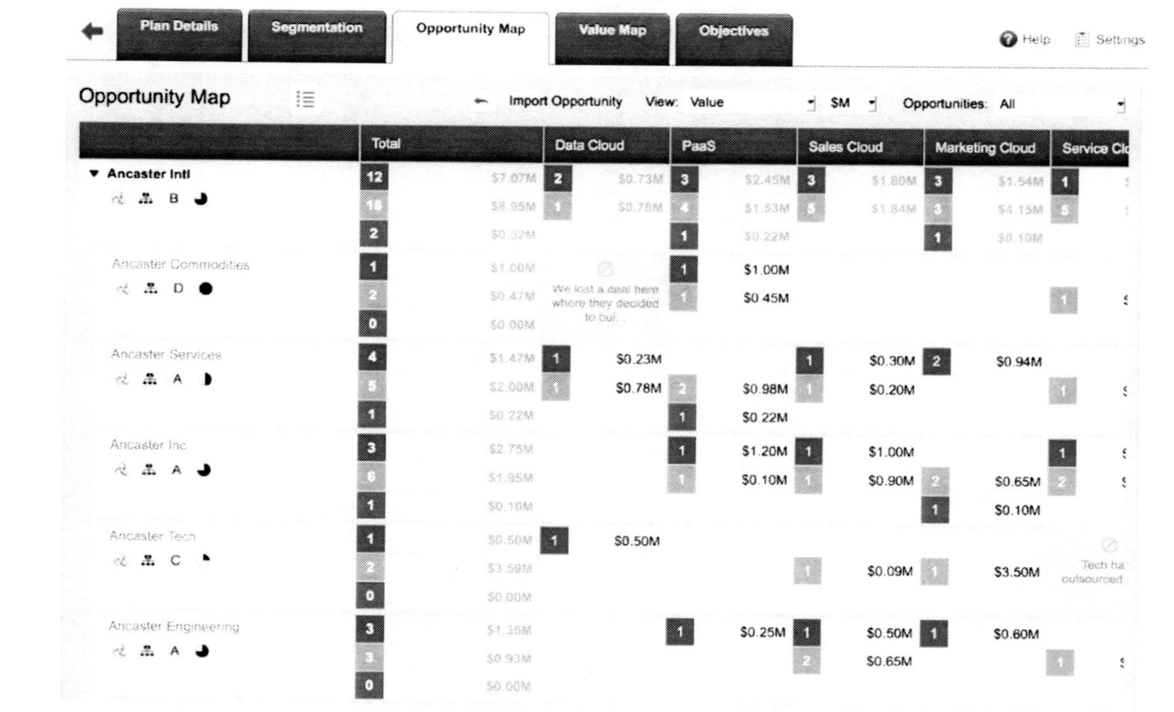

There are three main areas on the Opportunity Map:

1. **Solutions**: The columns on the map represent the Solutions you are selling to the account. This is the *what* you are selling.
2. **Plan Units**: On the left of the map is the list of Accounts or Business Units within the Account(s). This is *where* you are selling. Depending on whether you are creating an Account Plan for one large Account or for a number of smaller Accounts, a Plan Unit will be a Business Unit in the large Account, or a discrete account if you are building a multi-Account (or Portfolio) Account Plan. (In **Figure 38**, you will also notice a number of symbols beside each Plan Unit name. These relate to the Business Strategy Map, Political Map, Segmentation Quadrant and Level of Relationship that we discussed in earlier chapters.)
3. **Opportunities:** Your goal is to identify, create, and win opportunities at each intersection of Solutions and Plan Units – called Smart Intersections. On the Opportunity Map, you can record Potential, Current, and Won Opportunities, and identify White Space where you may have further opportunities.

To identify White Space and to uncover new Potential Opportunities, you should follow these simple steps:

1. Place all Won Opportunities on the Opportunity Map by correlating the relevant Solution(s) in the opportunity with the relevant Plan Unit.
2. Place all Current Opportunities on the Opportunity Map, again matching the Solution(s) in the opportunity with the Plan Unit with which you are engaged.

3. Identify the remaining White Space to explore Potential Opportunities.

Figure 39: The Opportunity Map – Detail (revised 2)

	Servers	Printing	Security
Acme US	$100,000	$80,000	White Space
Acme EMEA	White Space	White Space	$56,000
Acme APAC	$23,000	White Space	White Space

In the simple example we used at the start of the chapter, there were five areas of White Space. This is your opportunity to brainstorm with your team to come up with areas where you can convert an Unknown Need into a Known Need; and then to take that hypothesis to the customer.

For example, if Acme US had a need for Servers that resulted in a $100,000 opportunity for you, then you should ask yourself: What is it about their business requirement that might be similar in EMEA? Does the fact that there is a demand in EMEA for Security Consulting Services provide any insight in to the needs in the US or APAC? What Business Drivers, Initiatives or Critical Success Factors in EMEA or APAC might be positively impacted by the Printing Services solution that you have?

As I said at the outset of this chapter, now it is time to focus on the latter part of our Account Planning goal: *to create, develop, pursue, and win business that delivers mutual value.*

If you can shape the 'create' and 'develop' parts, then the 'pursue' and 'win' pieces get easier. Mapping your opportunities in the manner I described is the best way I know to illuminate the White Space and to focus the mind on creating new opportunities. Finding Potential Opportunities can be both very gratifying – you are really making a difference, creating, not just communicating, value – and also very financially rewarding.

When the customer says "Aha, I never thought of that – I think that could really help our company," then you know you might be on to something, and that is truly delivering on your potential.

Focus for Impact

When you do effective Account Planning, you should discover many new Potential Opportunities, as well as gather together all of your Current Opportunities. To maximize your return on effort, you need to focus on those that deliver the highest Mutual Value.

As a Trusted Advisor to your customers, you've invested a lot of time and effort in understanding their business profiles, the challenges they face or the Business Drivers that propel them to act, and you've helped them design Business Initiatives to address the challenges – you've even shaped the Critical Success Factors that they should focus on.

You've clearly added a lot of value. So, what do you get in return? Well, if the job was done well, you should now have a wealth of new Potential Opportunities that you can begin to work on with your customer.

And lest you get too excited too fast, the key word here is 'potential.' Opportunities created by you are by definition unqualified, and you need to choose carefully which ones to work on. Also, you must assess these opportunities alongside the Current Opportunities you are working.

There is no point in pursuing Potential Opportunities at the expense of not applying enough resource to progress your existing Current Opportunities unless, upon analysis, you determine that in fact you are chasing the wrong deals.

The key to selecting the right opportunities to target is a focus on Mutual Value: finding those opportunities that the customer really cares about and that will deliver maximum return to you. You can use the Value Map to find the relative Mutual Value of each opportunity to help you to determine where to focus. When you can find opportunities that provide strong Mutual Value, then you know that this is where you should focus.

As you can see from **Figure 40**, applying this Mutual Value assessment rigorously lets you see at a glance where you should choose to apply your efforts. You will note that this approach is similar to the model used in **CHAPTER 6: SEGMENT FOR PRIORITY** where you chose the optimum Business Units.

Now, using the Value Map you can place opportunities in each of the four quadrants. You need to determine the *Value to Us* and *Value to Customer* for each Current and Potential Opportunity to position the opportunity at the right place on the Value Map. Let's look at the factors that might help you to do that.

Figure 40: The Value Map

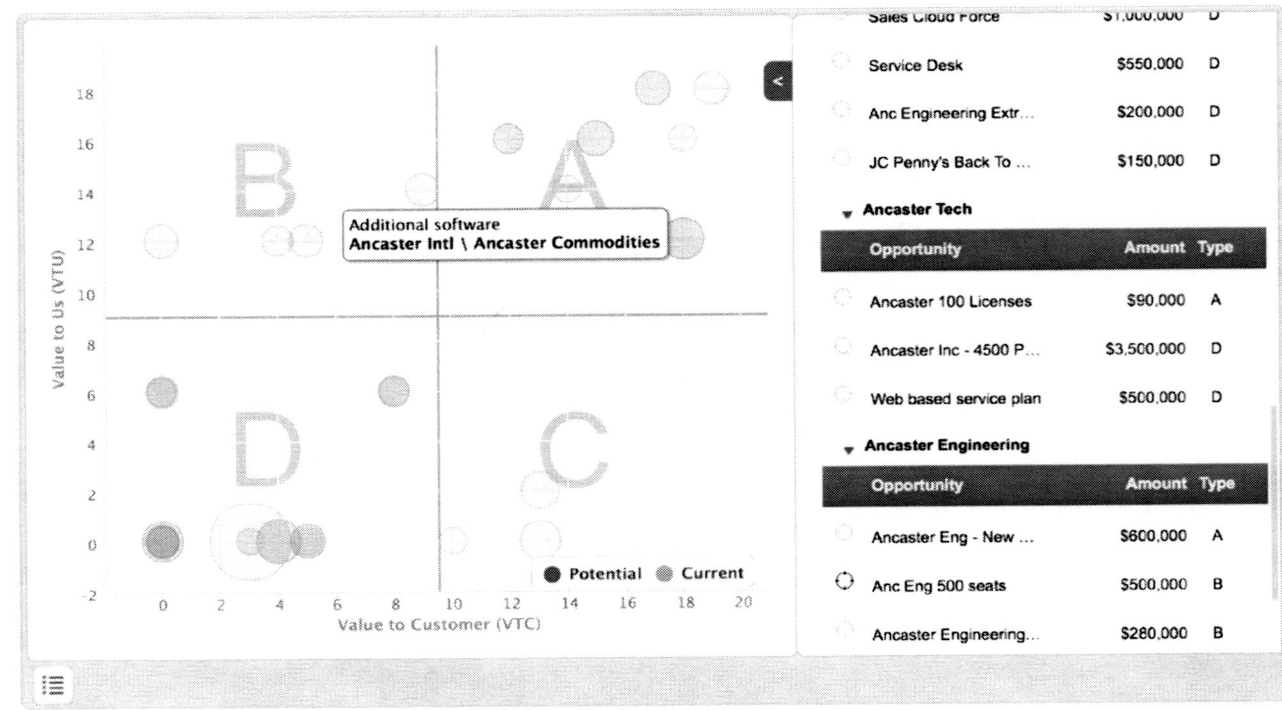

Value to Us

Value to Us can be defined as the benefit to your company in both the short-term and long-term. It measures the value of the opportunity at hand and the impact it will have on our future business.

Figure 41: Value to Us

Factor	Description	Good	Bad
Short-term Revenue	*What is the immediate revenue return from this opportunity?* When looking at short-term revenue you should consider the amount of the first sale and the date when you expect it to close. Short-term revenue is usually low in a Potential Opportunity but should be better in a Current Opportunity.	High	Low
Profitability	*How profitable is this opportunity?* Is this a profitable deal? Is there significant price pressure from competitors or the customer that will lead to heavy discounts that will have a negative impact on profitability?	High	Low
Future Revenue	*How much revenue are we likely to get in the future as a consequence of winning this opportunity?* What will this opportunity lead to in the future – over the next one to two years? Does this opportunity support your goals for the customer as a whole?	High	Low

Factor	Description	Goo d	Bad
Degree of Risk	*How much risk is there that your solution will not be successful?* Some things to consider when looking at the degree of risk are: What could cause our solution to fail? What are the critical dependencies in delivering value to the customer? How could the solution fail? What is the impact of failure on our relationship? What is the likelihood of failure after the sale?	Low	High
Strategic Value	*What is the strategic value of winning this opportunity?* In terms of strategic value, think about the value of the opportunity in the account over and above the actual value of the opportunity itself. How does this opportunity fit into your overall business plan? If you close this opportunity, will it advance your position in the industry? Will this customer bring help to you beyond financial value? Will the opportunity have true strategic value within the account? Will you learn from this opportunity in a way that will help improve your products or services?	High	Low

Value to Customer

Value to Customer can be defined very simply as how critical the initiative is to the enterprise's overall strategy. It relates to the customer's Business Initiative as opposed to the opportunity. All initiatives have some degree of importance; however, some are more important than others.

Figure 42: Value to the Customer

Factor	Description	Good	Bad
Revenue Growth	*What is the revenue growth associated with this initiative?* Often one of the highest drivers for action, how will the purchase of your solution drive revenue in the business? Will it provide considerable revenue growth? How do you know? Is your perspective on this aligned with that of your customer?	High	Low
Implementation Risk	*What is the risk that the implementation will fail?* Remember that, after a purchase, the risk shifts from you to the customer. One of the most common reasons for initiatives to stall is the fear of failure. How likely is it that this initiative might fail during implementation? The higher the risk (from the customer's perspective) the less attractive this opportunity will be.	Low	High
Cost Savings	*How much will the customer save by implementing your solution?* Can you project material cost savings from the related customer initiative that indicates that this opportunity will have a significant impact on the customer's bottom line?	High	Low

Factor	Description	Good	Bad
Customer Satisfaction Increase	*What is the (positive) impact on customer satisfaction that will result from this initiative?* Just like you the customer wants to increase its customer satisfaction rating. What impact will this initiative have on this measure?	High	Low
Compelling Event	*Is there a compelling event attached to this opportunity?* You know that a compelling event is a time-sensitive response to an internal or external pressure (Business Driver) connected to Key Players that drives the customer to act, to make a decision, to solve a problem or to take advantage of an opportunity in front of them by a defined date. Where a compelling event exists, the opportunity is a lot more attractive as it drives value for the customer in a defined period.	Strong	Weak

The answers to each of these questions will guide you to place the opportunities in the appropriate quadrant on the Value Map. If you are doing this manually, you might choose to weight each question and answer to help you to score the opportunities. Remember, you are looking for relative value, and should assess whether opportunity A is more valuable than opportunity B.

If you are using Dealmaker Smart Account Manager, the opportunities will be mapped automatically for you based on your answers to the questions (**Figure 43**). As a result:

Figure 43: The Value Map - Values

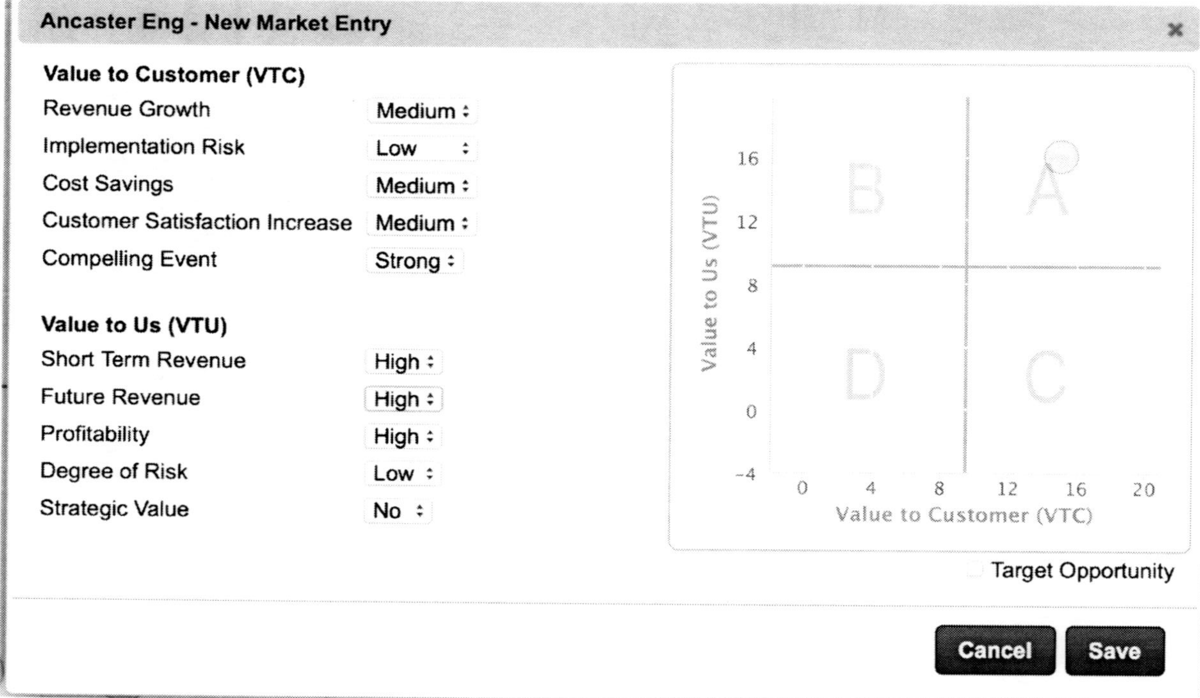

Ancaster Eng - New Market Entry
Value to Customer (VTC)
Revenue Growth
Medium
Implementation Risk
Low
Cost Savings
Medium
Customer Satisfaction Increase
Medium
Compelling Event
Strong
Value to Us (VTU)
Short Term Revenue
High
Future Revenue
High
Profitability
High
Degree of Risk
Low
Strategic Value
No
16
12
8
4
0
-4
0
4
8
12
16
20
Value to Us (VTU)
Value to Customer (VTC)
B
A
D
C
Target Opportunity
Cancel
Save

- Opportunities in the upper right quadrant of the map (the A quadrant) are of the highest value to both you and the customer.
- Opportunities in the upper left quadrant (the B quadrant) represent high value to you, but less to the customer.
- Opportunities in the lower right quadrant (the C quadrant) are high value to the customer, but less so for you,
- Opportunities in the lower left quadrant (the D quadrant) are of low value to you and the customer.

When you have set the values for each of the opportunities on the Value Map, it is likely that you will want to focus on a subset of the opportunities, to prioritize where you will allocate resources. In most cases, you should target those opportunities that end up in the A quadrant of the Value Map. Other opportunities are less likely to generate return for either you or the customer. Once you have selected the opportunities that you are going to invest in, you should apply that filter to your Opportunity Map to give you a clear picture of your planned activity in the account.

You can really solidify your vision of your account plan by discussing this Value Map with your customer. There's tremendous value in getting the customer's input to validate your assessment. It's good to get their feedback, as you look to monetize the work done to date, and start to see a return on your own investment of time and energy.

CHAPTER 10

EXECUTE THE PLAN

In their book, *Execution: The Discipline of Getting Things Done,* co-authors Larry Bossidy and Ram Charan essentially wrote that, "It's all in the execution." Years earlier Thomas Edison is reputed to have said "Vision without execution is hallucination." One of my early observations of the sales methodology industry was that it was very hard for sales professionals to execute on their Opportunity Plan or Account Plan. There was lots of valuable teaching on the strategy to use, but very little support on the practical execution. Very few companies had managed to embed their sales methodology in the everyday workings of their business. That was why we developed Dealmaker. Developing your plan has limited benefit unless you have a clear execution path to follow, and the requisite discipline, stamina and tools to follow through on the plan.

If you've made it to here – you've done a lot of work. You clearly have the discipline and the stamina. Now I will spell out how to convert all of that good work into an Execution Plan that you and your Account Team can deliver.

The three themes we started with back in **CHAPTER 1: WHY ACCOUNT PLANNING MATTERS** were *Research for Insight, Integrate for Velocity* and *Focus for Impact*. I want you to keep these themes to the forefront of your mind as you finalize the plan that you need to execute to reap the rewards of all of your hard work:

- **Research for Insight:** In **CHAPTER 4: RESEARCH FOR INSIGHT**, I introduced the concept of Account Planning as strategic business planning applied on an individual customer basis. By the time you finished that chapter, you may have felt a little brow-beaten, as I continued to hark on the need for continuous research. Hopefully at this stage in the book, you've come to see the value in spending enough time sharpening the axe before you start to cut down the tree with a blunt instrument. Research, as you know, is not limited to the customer. It must also encompass all of the Three Cs: Customer, Competitor and Company. You learned that you should slow down your natural inclination to pursue deals now. If you do your homework on the Account, and apply the experience you have gained from working with other customers, you should be able to bring insight to the customer. If you don't do the research, then you won't have the knowledge, and then you can't bring insight – and that is a missed opportunity. Your role is to create value for the customer, not just to communicate information about your company or your solutions. Before you position your value, a prerequisite is having a deep sense of what the customer values. When you have done your research, you can begin to feel comfortable in the customer's shoes, and begin the walk together toward Mutual Value.
- **Integrate for Velocity:** In **CHAPTER 5: INTEGRATE FOR VELOCITY**, I set out the four primary sources of input to your Account Plan that you needed to integrate to achieve maximum velocity.

- Existing CRM data in Salesforce.
- Knowledge of the Account Team.
- Information shared by the customer.
- Supplementary data from research sources such as Data.com.

You learned that, without a centralized way to manage the plan, velocity and effectiveness suffer. Integrating your team and the customer with the data in Salesforce and the pertinent data from supplementary data sources is the only way to provide a single sharable resource. With that resource you can maximize organizational velocity, Account Team velocity, and revenue velocity.

- **Focus for Impact:** Focus is the parallel thread that runs alongside Mutual Value from the beginning to the end of this book. It is in fact the catalyst for Mutual Value, driving you to uncover areas that benefit you and the customer. In **CHAPTER 6: SEGMENT FOR PRIORITY**, I showed how to prioritize the Plan Units in your Account Plan to focus on where you can uniquely and competitively deliver maximum value. Then in **CHAPTER 9: FOCUS FOR IMPACT**, you saw again how you had to make some hard choices to target the opportunities on which to focus – those that deliver Mutual Value.

These three principles remain constant and should continue to be your compass as you plot your course through Plan Execution.

As you become master of your plan, you're also on your way to becoming a leader in your own marketplace. You have segmented and prioritized the Plan Units in your Account Plan. In understanding the customer's decision process, you've also learned about your role in that process, and the level of relationship that applies in different circumstances.

You've explored Business Drivers, Business Initiatives and Critical Success Factors as your guide to how you might align your offerings with the customer's needs. That pointed you in the direction of Potential Opportunities, which along with Current Opportunities, you learned to prioritize using the Value Map.

That's a lot of progress. You're really getting to understand your target market, and you've learned about what is motivating the customer to act, and that's a great value accelerator.

You're making headway but you're not quite finished. You don't want your Account Plan to become Edison's hallucination. No, you are going to plough through to the end, to make sure that you benefit from the opportunity you have created. Otherwise it would be a lost opportunity.

The world is an increasingly chaotic place and you have very little time. So, sometimes you might be tempted to think that you don't have the time to plan. Planning might take time – but what it also does is provide a framework for a concerted approach to a task – particularly in scenarios where more than one person is involved in executing the task.

Major Account Teams plan in order to orchestrate their own performance. By nature, Account Planning is a team discipline: not just the team inside of your organization and the various members who launch the marketing strategy, but also the teams in your customer organizations. All of the resources of your business are brought to bear on the Account according to one script, owned and maintained by the Account Team. And that script is the plan. So planning is something that allows you to behave proactively in the account because you're writing the script. Imagine trying to orchestrate your resources, marketing, customer relationships, and partners in a goal-oriented fashion without a plan. You would waste valuable time and resources – most likely never achieving your goal.

Here are some of the benefits you should expect from your plan:

- Information to create **alignment** between your actions and your customer's business objectives.
- Insight to see where the **new opportunities** are within your account, and to track the actions taken to pursue those opportunities.
- Demonstration of your **professionalism** through deep understanding of the customer's needs.
- **Justification** to secure scarce resources from your management.
- A script that allows **co-ordination** among your team in goal-oriented fashion.
- A **communication** tool for new people who join your team, helping them quickly to understand your customer's business needs, culture, and key relationships.
- **Simplification** of your Account by clearly outlining the actions you need to take in order to achieve your goal.

Finally, if you have deployed Dealmaker Smart Account Manager in Salesforce, your plan is always-on, integrated and up-to-date, and as you gain evidence of progress you will maintain confidence in your approach and feel a sense of reward for the time you spend planning.

The Execution Planning Framework

I'm sure you'd love to have the ability to see into the future, to have magical glasses that let you see around corners, anticipate what's coming next, and peek under the covers of your destiny before you set off. I don't think that the Execution Planning framework (**Figure 44**) quite achieves that, but it helps to lay out the roadmap to plan the journey.

Figure 44: The Execution Planning Framework

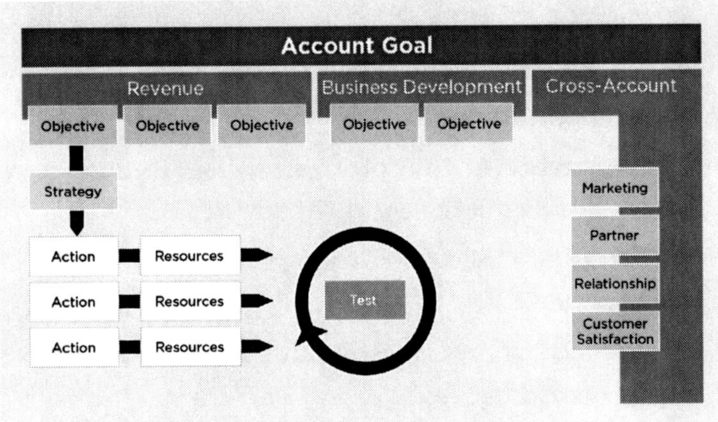

Once you have identified the goal for your account, you need to define your objectives to help you to achieve that goal. Objectives, combined with related Strategies and Actions, are the very directional signposts that point to the attainment of your goal. Experienced practitioners realize that an OSA (pronounced Oh-Sa) becomes your friend, your travelling companion, always there to keep you on track and as a constant monitor of your progress. A plan without its OSAs is just a plan, while a plan with OSAs becomes a business plan that you can execute against.

Let's start with Objectives. Your objectives describe what you need to achieve in order to reach your Account Goal, and can be described in three categories:

- **Revenue Objectives:** Current Opportunities that you are pursuing need a Revenue Objective. You should have one for each Plan Unit that you have selected, focusing on the combined revenue from your Current Opportunities in that unit over the Account Plan period.
- **Business Development Objective:** Every Plan Unit that has a Potential Opportunity needs a Business Development Objective that focuses on qualifying, in the short term, your future opportunities.
- **Cross-Account Objectives:** In addition to Revenue and Business Development Objectives that apply specifically to opportunities or Plan Units, you also might require broader objectives that apply either to the Plan Unit, or to all of the Plan Units that you have included in your plan. These objectives ensure that you utilize **all** of the resources available to you to effectively maximize your position.

I know you know this already, but it is worth calling it out: each objective must be S.M.A.R.T.:

- **Specific:** The more precise you can be with the definition of your Objective, the easier it will be to understand. For example, if I said that my Objective is "to be salesforce.com's preferred partner," it might be unclear as to what that means exactly. On the other hand, if I said I want "to be their preferred partner for Account Planning software," you can understand immediately what that means.

- **Measurable:** The consequence of specificity is ease of measurement. If I am the preferred Account Planning software partner for salesforce.com, then more of their customers should use Dealmaker Smart Account Manager than any other solution. That is easy to measure.
- **Achievable:** However, your objective can be specific and measurable and still be way out of the bounds of reality. For a plan to be an effective script of performance, every Objective, Strategy, and Action has to be achievable. So you have to constantly ask yourself: Can this be accomplished, given the resource constraints? What is the likelihood of success, given my ability to orchestrate these resources and move them in a given amount of time?
- **Relevant:** Everything also needs to be relevant. Remember that by the end of this process you will have a fairly large number of Actions after you have identified your Goal, Objectives, and Strategies. You want to weed out every single Action that is not relevant to achieving your Objectives or your Account Goal.
- **Time-bounded:** In addition you must consider the time it will take you and have a documented target date for completion.

Revenue Objectives

Revenue Objectives relate to Current Opportunities in Plan Units that you have chosen to work in your plan. In each case you need to consider the total revenue, the Strategy that will describe your approach, the Actions that need to happen, with the associated resources that are required. In summary, you then have your Objective, Strategy and Actions (OSA).

Figure 45 shows an example of a clear SMART objective, where you have decided on strategy and called out the specific actions to be taken, with defined resource and target timelines. This now gives everyone a clear picture of their role and inter-dependencies. If you have put thought into the objectives and strategies with the team, you will come up with good ideas that will help you to overcome any issues, even when you think the odds are stacked against you.

She said to me that she'll reach her objective
No matter what they said
She would not be affected
They wouldn't believe her ideas were rejected
She was dejected
She said she'd find a way so forget about them
Odds were stacked against
But she wouldn't give in
Wouldn't give in.

Objective, from the album Mighty by The Planet Smashers, 2003. Printed with permission from Stomp Records.

Figure 45: Revenue Objective, Strategy and Actions

Plan Unit	**Medical Devices EMEA**		
Revenue Objective	Sell and implement DW2000, Professional Services, and Security Servers for a total value of $1.7m before the end of the second quarter to provide the implementation services team in Medical Devices EMEA with the ability to reduce production malfunctions by 30%.		
Strategy	By developing and executing a complete Opportunity Plan, we can gain agreement on the production malfunction challenges, supported by evidence, to solidify the compelling event, employ the right competitive strategy, and develop the necessary relationships with key players to win the business.		
Action Plan			
Action	**Resources**	**Date**	**Owner**
Develop Opportunity plan for DW2000 $350k opportunity and supporting Pro Services $150k	King, DW Support	4/30	Eric King
Develop Opportunity plan for Security Servers $1.2m opportunity	Ray, Security Product Manager	5/30	Stevie Ray
Develop reference case studies	King, Marketing	6/15	Eric King
Solidify Exec Relationship with VP Alb Collins	King, EBC, Trent	6/21	Eric King

Business Development Objectives

Your Business Development Objectives summarize the specific areas in your Account that you want to pursue, based on the Potential Opportunities you have identified. They may be written around a specific offering, and / or several Plan Units where there are common opportunities. The Strategy that supports your Business Development Objective focuses on how you will investigate or qualify the Potential Opportunities you've identified. The idea is that once qualified, your Business Development Objectives will provide input to Revenue Objectives.

The Actions you identify are the major steps you need to take in order to achieve your Strategy and, of course, will need to have the associated resources that you will identify to carry out the tasks. These may include specific team members, marketing programs, executive involvement, or funding you need in order to support your Actions.

Business Development Objectives are sometimes harder to complete than Revenue Objectives. By definition they are less tangible and require sustained commitment to the long-term vision of the plan.

The strategy that you employ is critical. A well-crafted strategy for a Business Development Objective will:

- Identify how you will achieve your Objective.
- Enable you to prioritize your resources.
- Provide common direction for the Account Team.

Figure 46: Business Development Objective, Strategy and Actions

Plan Unit	**Nutritionals Global**		
Business Development Objective	Identify and qualify two opportunities for any of DW2000, Professional Services, and Security Servers in one or more of the Nutritionals Global facilities in the next three months.		
Strategy	Discover and assess existing Business Initiatives, and determine whether our solutions are applicable. Brainstorm new possible initiatives based on Nutritionals market insights.		
Action Plan			
Action	**Resources**	**Date**	**Owner**
Identify key contacts and initiate plan to gain meeting to discover existing business insights	King	5/12	Eric King
Research Nutritionals market insights	King, Market Analysts	6/11	Eric King
Brainstorm solution fit and new possible initiatives	Account Team, Customer sponsor	6/30	Eric King
Create presentation to capture hypothesis and possible business impact	Account Team, Marketing	7/12	Eric King

Discipline is important. You need to watch out for any lack of understanding or agreement, be clear on how completion of actions will be monitored, and of course make sure that you have the commitment of everyone on the team.

Figure 47: Objectives

Objectives

Plan Unit: Show All

Description	Plan Unit	Type	Strategy	Owner	Actions
▶ Over the next 4 to 6 months, verify Ancaster Engineering's global software needs and position ourselves as the most capable global delivery organization for their long-term software investments (est. $3m to $4m).	Ancaster Engineering	Revenue	by gaining in-depth Ancaster Engineering business knowledge and by leveraging our presence in other AI units to establish our leading-edge capabilities with the Ancaster Engineering management team.	Brian Rice	1 / 2 ✕
▶ In next 4 to 5 months, confirm Ancaster International's expansion plans (estimated at $0.5 to $1m in hardware) for this year and establish our unique delivery capabilities with their executive decision makers.	Ancaster International	Business Development	by sharing with them our understanding of their key business drivers and asking them to validate or alter the initiatives and CSFs that we think will resonate with their business.	Brian Rice	1 / 2 ✕
▼ Identify 3 opportunities in next 3 months to initiate consulting projects in the 2 open Business Units of AI.	Ancaster Inc	Marketing	by focusing our consulting practice team on investigating and qualifying the consulting needs of Ancaster Services and Ancaster Commodities	Brian Rice	2 / 4 ✕

Action	Description	Owner	Priority	Status	Due Date	
look for key contact list	Identify key contact list for 2 Business Units and set a plan to gain introductions. Javier has contacts in the other Units who have invested in consulting with us.	Brian Rice	Normal	Waiting on someone else	11/21/2012	✕
Develop presentation	Develop comprehensive presentation to demonstrate consulting capabilities. Requires scoping of marketing resources.	Brian Rice	Normal	In Progress	11/22/2012	✕
References	Line up consulting reference calls in other AI divisions.	Brian Rice	High	Completed	10/17/2012	✕

One of the best ways to maximize the likelihood of success is to make it easy for all participants to contribute, collaborate and communicate. This harks back to one of the key principles I set out earlier: Integrate for Velocity.

Figure 47 shows how your OSAs might be captured in Dealmaker Smart Account Manager in Salesforce. This is a good example of how you might want to maximize the effectiveness of OSA management.

Getting Help from Others

Now that you have completed your Revenue and Business Development Objectives, you need to step back and consider the broader aspects of the Account. While most of your efforts will focus eventually on finding Current and Potential Opportunities, limiting the scope of your thinking to that narrow perspective can give a blinkered view. Opportunities happen in the context of the business. The business operates in the context of its market, and is stewarded by its leadership and management team. These multiple facets color the landscape in which you are operating. When you can, you will need to leverage other resources to add a little biased tint to those shades.

I get by with a little help from my friends.

With a Little Help from My Friends, Sgt. Pepper's Lonely Hearts Club Band, Beatles, 1967

One of the advances in modern maritime travel is the application of technology to create a reduction in the number of people needed to steer, propel, and maintain a ship. It used to be that the sails had to be rigged by hand, the ropes tightened, and the whole thing kept 'ship-shape' by countless sailors.

Navigating an Account Plan is like that. There are varied and specialized tasks to do, coverage to maintain, and many existing services involved. The good news is that you're not alone trying to do everything – there are different internal departments, partners and others that all share your vested interest in creating success.

Integral to your own ability to succeed will be how you work with these other teams and groups. Part of that is to identify who they are. Sometime that is easy to do. It is usually obvious that you should leverage your own Marketing department. Other times though it can be more difficult either to recognize the need for external assistance, or to conceive of situations where perhaps a partner might help. Knowing who you can count on – and should be aware of in the Account to potentially ally with – is a key aspect of creating a successful approach to the account.

There are few distinct viewpoints in business that are as polarized as those of marketing and sales professionals. Marketing folks decry the poor sales conversion and sales people abhor what they characterize as the risible value delivered by expensive marketing.

In truth this tension – though sometimes understandable – misses the point. On today's playing field, successful selling, and the leading sales professionals, encapsulate the best of strategic marketing, but at an individual customer level. Integrated sales and marketing guides the customer through a logical sequence from awareness to action.

Marketing is a perfect example of where you might develop a Cross-Account Objective. Whether you are just trying to gain initial recognition in the Account or in a specific

Plan Unit, hoping that the customer might begin to care about your solution, or shaping the customer's inclination towards a specific product selection, you would be well advised to leverage marketing to further your efforts.

I categorize the effect that marketing and sales can have in a customer interaction into four distinct phases:

- Awareness.
- Interest.
- Preference.
- Action.

First you need to utilize marketing to help you to create *awareness*. If the business you are targeting is not aware of your products and solutions, it's going to be hard to sell anything. When the customer is aware of her potential need for your products or services, then her *interest* grows. The next step is to create *preference*. You want to be her preferred choice. This is where sales and marketing work together to create valued differentiation – your unique business value. Once you have established yourself as being the preferred choice, the next step is *action* and it's your job to help the customer make a decision, or recommendation, or place an order.

As you can see in **Figure 48**, the level of involvement and responsibility transitions from marketing to sales as you progress through these stages.

Marketing is an effective companion as you navigate your way through your Execution Plan. You need to determine how to best apply this valuable resource to support your Goals in the Account and help you attain your Revenue Objective.

Figure 48: The Interaction of Marketing and Sales

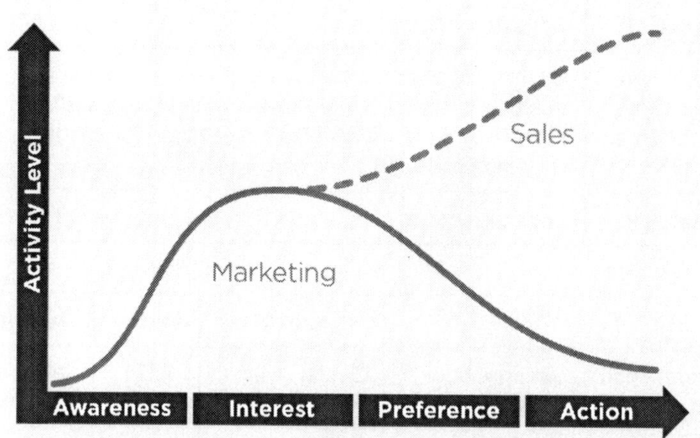

To be successful, you must effectively utilize every resource available to you if you are to maximize impact. One such key resource is Marketing – and it needs to be integrated with your sales efforts. In this simple example of a Marketing OSA (**Figure 49**), you are preparing to create awareness and interest across the Account by leveraging social media and thought leadership activities. Typically these will sit with Marketing, and if you were to do all of these activities yourself you would have less time to spend selling, or discovering new Potential Opportunities in the account.

Marketing is one example of the 'Others' who might help you. Partners, analysts, other customers, and the customer herself can each be channeled to support Objectives that you determine will help advance your cause.

Account Planning is team support. It's up to you to figure out the plays and get each player in the right spot. It takes discipline and effort but I promise you, that if you execute well, the results will be dramatic.

Figure 49: Marketing Objectives, Strategies and Actions

Plan Unit	**Organic Products**		
Marketin g Objective	By the end of next quarter create awareness of our position in the Security Server marketplace with at least two of the executives responsible for security at Organic Products		
Strategy	Leverage social media and thought leadership program		
Action Plan			
Action	**Resources**	**Date**	**Owner**
Validate contact information and get social contact profile for each exec. Follow each on Twitter, LinkedIn etc. Engage with their social media activity.	Social Marketing Unit	4/17	Jane Raitt
Invite James Brown, Vicki Estevez, Henry Johnson to our Security Leaders Summit	Eric King	3/18	Eric King
Deliver custom 'white paper' to Organic	Jane Writer		Eric King
Ask Tom Harrison at Organic to ask the exec leaders to participate in Security Benchmark Study	David Matthews		David Matthews

And Finally

Last of the Independents is a song by Rory Gallagher from Photo-Finish, his seventh studio album. Gallagher was recognized as a free spirit, an individual thinker, who often took a path that others chose to ignore.

I am the last of the independents
I play by my own rules

Last of the Independents, Photo-Finish, Rory Gallagher, 1978

Account Planning is not a discipline practiced by the mediocre. You will need to separate yourself from the crowd, and apply a little independent thinking to achieve the benefits that accrue from rigorous application of this discipline.

© Rik Walton

Rory Gallagher was one of the greatest blues guitarists of all time. Rory was born in Ballyshannon, County Donegal, in Ireland, and grew up in Cork (my home town) in the south of Ireland.

Many modern day musicians, including The Edge from U2, Slash of Guns N' Roses, Johnny Marr of The Smiths, Davy Knowles, Janick Gers of Iron Maiden, Glenn Tipton of Judas Priest, Brian May of Queen, Vivian Campbell of Def Leppard, Gary Moore, and Joe Bonamassa, cite Gallagher as an inspiration in their formative musical years.

From the age of seven, Rory researched every scrap of blues music he could find, integrated his Irishness with Chicago Blues, Delta Blues and any other kind of blues he could find to produce his own unique guitar sound. Then he focused on what he excelled at – playing live, loud and fast.

Research. Integrate. Focus. Now there's a coincidence. Didn't we talk about these three points back in **CHAPTER 1: WHY ACCOUNT PLANNING MATTERS**?

Thanks for reading.

PLAYLIST

As I said early in the book, no one likes to plan. It is hard work and needs discipline and effort. Account Planning is important, but sometimes, when you're in the early stages it feels that it will be an uphill struggle. Having read the book, I hope you agree that it is worthwhile. I'd like to think that this book makes it easier for you – and I hope that you found at least some parts easy to consume and easy to apply.

I borrowed from the songs in this book to lighten the load, and provide a little color. If you find yourself humming along, or remembering a song long forgotten, or even practicing your air guitar moves, then I have succeeded in my objective – to add some fun and the occasional distraction, to make the journey more entertaining.

As the profits from this book go to the WITNESS charity, I would like to have included some songs from Peter Gabriel. Peter founded WITNESS 20 years ago, and if you are not familiar with WITNESS you should check out their website (www.witness.org). The work they do is very important in our world today. Perhaps *Don't Give Up* from Peter's So album might have been appropriate, or *Games Without Frontiers* from Melt, or maybe *Digging in the Dirt* from Us may well be more applicable. In any case, familiarize yourself with

Peter's music and WITNESS. I think you will find both to be uplifting.

Now, on to the songs in the book. First, it is important to say that all of the rights in the lyrics belong to the composers, or their respective publishers – and, as The TAS Group is in the intellectual property business itself, it is important to recognize that. If you're prompted to explore some of the songs in the book that you've not encountered before, then please buy them and support these great artists as they continue to enrich our lives.

The Playlist and the Players

Barbra Streisand

♪	*People*	People, 1964	Page 119

People, the title track from the eponymous album, was a newly recorded version of the hit from the Broadway musical *Funny Girl* in which Streisand stars. More middle of the road than the rest of the songs in this list, *People* is however a timeless classic, and you probably know it already. It belongs in your music collection.

The Beatles

♪	*With a Little Help From My Friends*	Sgt. Pepper's Lonely Hearts Club Band, 1967	Page 178

There is not a lot that has not been said about The Beatles, probably the most commercially successful and critically acclaimed act in the history of popular music. This song, originally from *Sgt. Pepper's Lonely Heart Club Band* was released in 1967. Personally I am a fan of the Joe Cocker version with the raspiness in his voice adding a depth to the song even beyond that original recording. Joe Cocker is the blues-rock singer who came to prominence in the 1960s with his passionate cover of this song. It was the title track of Cocker's first album, released in 1969, and still stands the test of time.

Bob Dylan

♪	*Gotta Serve Somebody*	Slow Train Coming, 1979	Page 93

Bob Dylan is one of the greats, an American singer-songwriter, author, poet and artist. He has written some great songs that in many cases reached the height of their fame when covered by other artists. The most recent example of this is Adele's version of *Make You Feel My Love* on her 2008 album *19*. I first came across *Gotta Serve Somebody* on Etta James' *Matriarch of the Blues* album, and that is still my favorite version of the song.

Cheap Trick

♪	*I Want You To Want Me*	In Color, 1977	Page 151
♪	*Stiff Competition*	Heaven Tonight, 1978	Page 59
♪	*I Know What I Want*	Dream Police, 1979	Page 148

Here's a band that is still going strong nearly 40 years after they started. Cheap Trick is an American rock band that was formed in 1973. Their longevity is a testament to the addictive nature of their songs. *Heaven Tonight* is regarded by many as their best album, and is certainly a good introduction to Cheap Trick for novices. The band has been very successful in Japan where they are frequently referred to as the 'American Beatles,' and they are well known for their four decades of almost continuous touring.

Eurythmics

♪	*Sweet Dreams*	Sweet Dreams (are made of this), 1983	Page 120

If you are not familiar with the exquisite voice of Annie Lennox, half of the British pop music duo Eurythmics, there is joy in your future. Eurythmics was Annie Lennox and Dave Stewart, who worked together from 1980 to 1990. *Sweet Dreams* is arguably their signature song, and certainly their most successful. With 75 million record sales worldwide, this is a band well worth investigating.

Larry Williams

♪	*Slow Down*	1958	Page 23

Slow Down is a 24-bar blues song written and performed by Larry Williams. It was released as a single as the B-side of *Dizzy Miss Lizzy*. Both of these songs were later covered by The Beatles. *Slow Down* was performed or released by Led Zeppelin, The Jam, The Flamin' Groovies, Golden Earring and Brian May of Queen. You can buy the 7-inch vinyl recording of *Slow Down / Dizzy Miss Lizzy* on Amazon.

Metallica

♪	*Nothing Else Matters*	Metallica, 1992	Page 51

The first time I saw Metallica live was in 2011 at Dreamforce, salesforce.com's annual conference. *Nothing Else Matters* is a beautiful power ballad penned by James Hetfield, the band's singer and rhythm guitarist. The B-Side of the single was *Enter Sandman,* a hard-hitting metal song more typical of Metallica's other work. If you're not familiar with Metallica, but know what I mean when I say "turn it up to 11," then you have a treat in store.

The Planet Smashers

♪	*Objective*	Mighty, 2003	Page 173

I only came across The Planet Smashers quite recently, and I was very happy to find they had a song that fitted right in with the Objectives part of the book. This is a very enjoyable band. Formed in 1994, and based in Montreal, The Planet Smashers are a ska punk outfit somewhat reminiscent of the English band Madness. Well worth checking out.

Rose Royce

♪	*Love Don't Live Here Anymore*	Rose Royce III: Strikes Again!, 1978	Page 39

Songwriter Miles Gregory wrote this song while undergoing medical treatment, and that situation and his deteriorating physical health became the inspiration behind the song. If you recall the original version by Rose Royce, you will remember it as one of the early effective uses of the Electronic Linn Drum machine. (Am I getting too nerdy now?) It is a great song and has been covered by many artists including Morrissey, Mary J. Blige, and, perhaps most notably, by Madonna on her 1984 *Like A Virgin* album.

Rory Gallagher

♪	*A Million Miles Away*	Tattoo, 1973 / Irish Tour '74, 1974	
♪	*The Last of the Independents*	Photo-Finish, 1978	Page 182

Although the first song above is not the song included in the book, this is the song I wanted to bring to your attention. I attended Rory Gallagher's funeral in Cork in Ireland in 1995, and I remember Lou Martin, Rory's one-time keyboard player, playing this song in the church during the packed service. The song appeared on *Tattoo* and also on *Irish Tour '74* – my favorite version. One of the world's greatest rock and blues guitarists, Rory has a wealth of recordings just waiting to be discovered by those who are new to his music. This particular song is at once evocative and blistering, soulful and rampant, and a pleasure to hear. During his short life, Rory played with Muddy Waters, Jerry Lee Lewis, Albert King, Lonnie Donegan, Peter Green, Eric Burdon, Jack Bruce, Slash and many others. If you don't have any Rory Gallagher in your music collection, you should start with *Irish Tour '74* and go from there. If you already have some of Rory's music, then you know what I mean.

U2

♪	*I Still Haven't Found What I'm Looking For*	The Joshua Tree, 1987	Page 148

Coincidentally, in 1996, the first *Annual Rory Gallagher Musician Award* went to The Edge, the guitarist with Irish mega-band U2. Formed as a teenage band with possibly limited musical proficiency at that time, U2 were to explode on the scene just four years later with their debut album *Boy*. By the time *The Joshua Tree* was released they were well-established, but it took this album, the band's fifth, to produce their first number-one hits in the US with *I Still Haven't Found What I'm Looking For* and *With Or Without You*. U2 has since gone on from strength to strength and occasionally earned the band the position as number one in the world. Not bad for a little band from Ireland!

Permissions

I am grateful for permission to reproduce lyrics from the playlist as follows:

People
Words by Bob Merrill, Music by Jule Styne. Copyright © 1963 (renewed) Chappell-Styne, Inc. (ASCAP) and Wonderful Music, Inc. (ASCAP). All rights administered by Chappell & Co., Inc. All rights reserved.

With a Little Help From My Friends
Words and music by John Lennon and Paul McCartney. Copyright © 1965. Reproduced by permission of Sony ATV Music Publishing Ltd., London W1F 9LD.

I Want You To Want Me
Words and music by Rick Nielsen. Copyright© 1977 (renewed 2005), 1978 Screen Gems-EMI Music, Inc. and Adult Music. All rights controlled and administered by Screen Gems-EMI Music Inc.All rights reserved. International copyright secured. Used by permission.Reprinted by permission of Hal Leonard Corporation. Reproduced by permission of Screen Gems-EMI Music Ltd., London W1F 9LD.

Stiff Competition
Words and music by Rick Nielsen. Copyright © 1979 Screen Gems-EMI Music Inc. and Adult Music.All rights controlled and administered by Screen Gems-EMI Music Inc. All rights reserved. International copyright secured. Used by permission. Reprinted by permission of Hal Leonard Corporation. Reproduced by permission of Screen Gems-EMI Music Ltd., London W1F 9LD.

I Know What I Want
Words and music by Rick Nielsen. Copyright © 1979 Screen Gems-EMI Music Inc. and Adult Music. All rights controlled and administered by Screen Gems-EMI Music Inc. All rights reserved. International copyright secured. Used by permission. Reprinted by permission of Hal Leonard Corporation. Reproduced by permission of Screen Gems-EMI Music Ltd., London W1F 9LD.

Sweet Dreams (Are Made Of This)
Words and music by Annie Lennox and David Stewart. Copyright © 1983 Universal Music Publishing MGB Ltd. All rights in the US and Canada administered by Universal Music – MGB Songs. International copyright secured. All rights reserved. Reprinted by permission of Hal Leonard Corporation.

Slow Down
Words and music by Larry Williams.Copyright © 1957 (renewed) by Arc Music Corporation (BMI) and Larina Music (BMI).Worldwide rights for Arc Music Corporation owned by Arc/Conrad Music LLC (administered by BMG Rights Management (US) LLC).All rights reserved. Used by permission. Reproduced by permission of Sony ATV Music Publishing Ltd., London W1F 9LD.

Nothing Else Matters
Words and music by James Hetfield and Lars Ulrich. Copyright © 1991 Creeping Death Music (ASCAP). International copyright secured. All rights reserved. Reprinted by permission of Cherry Lane Music Company. Reprinted by permission of Hal Leonard Corporation. Reprinted by permission of King, Holmes, Paterno & Berliner.

Objective
From the album *Mighty* by The Planet Smashers 2003. Printed with permission from Stomp Records.

Love Don't Live Here Anymore
Words and Music by Miles Gregory. Copyright © 1978 Warner-Tamerlane Publishing Corp. (BMI) and May Twelfth Music (BMI). All rights administered by Warner-Tamerlane Publishing Corp. All rights reserved.

The Last of The Independents
Words and music by Rory Gallagher. Copyright © 1979 Strange Music Ltd. All rights reserved. International copyright secured. Used by permission of Music Sales Limited.

If you have read as far as here, then you are seriously interested in music. If you are, then I guarantee that you will find something new here to enjoy. For now – better get back to your Account Planning work!

RESOURCES

Blog: Dealmaker 365 (www.dealmaker365.com)

I have a fundamental belief that Sales makes the world go around, and that sales professionals are underserved when it comes to professional training and development. I don't believe the traditional sales training model works, and I think dramatic improvements can be made. In this blog, I offer my thoughts, for what they're worth, and I welcome debate and discussion. You will find The TAS Group's company blog at www.thetasgroup.com/blog.

Twitter: @dealmaker365

If you would like to follow me on Twitter, @dealmaker365 is my Twitter handle. You also might want to follow The TAS Group @thetasgroup.

YouTube Channel: DealmakerMagic (www.youtube.com/dealmakermagic)

Here you will find various videos of interviews, conference presentations and Dealmaker demos.

Instant Sales Process: Dealmaker Genius (www. dealmakergenius.com)

Dealmaker Genius is a free resource that helps sales professionals to create their own customized sales processes. Dealmaker Genius removes critical barriers to success by enabling anyone, anywhere, to improve their performance by creating a high-quality sales process. In 15 minutes or less you can create your own sales process, customized to your company, products and services – aligned with how your customers buy. Once you create your sales process, you can share it with your colleagues.

Sales Benchmarking: Dealmaker Index (www. dealmakerindex.com)

Another free resource, Dealmaker Index is the world's first global measure of sales effectiveness for companies and individual sales professionals. Based on an analysis of 92 sales performance factors, mapped against proven successful approaches, Dealmaker Index measures the effectiveness of sales organizations and sales individuals across areas such as deal close rates, sales cycle management, value creation and sales opportunity development. It analyzes their activities, behaviors and attitudes and their strategic alignment with their companies and the resulting sales velocity they can achieve. It then produces a detailed custom sales performance success roadmap for both individuals and companies.

The TAS Group Resources (www.thetasgroup.com/resources)

The resource page on The TAS Group's website provides a wealth of information. Here you can find an extensive library of white papers, webinar archives, customer case studies, links to analyst reports, social network activity, and much more.

ACKNOWLEDGEMENTS

The 'writing part' of a book is a solitary task, but the 'getting it right' part takes an army. I have been blessed with lots of support, for which I am truly appreciative.

Throughout the process others toiled selflessly to improve my work; the core content, the design, the writing, the references, the proof reading, the lyrics, the copyright permissions, the layout, and the flow. Without their help **ACCOUNT PLANNING *in* SALESFORCE** would never have happened.

Many of my collaborators in this effort are colleagues from The TAS Group, a company I have been privileged to lead since 2005. Some are co-travelers in the sales effectiveness industry who share a similar vision of the end destination: a better way to make sales people more productive. Representatives of our customers also willingly gave their time to help shape the outcome and joined me in this endeavor. My friends and partners at salesforce.com were tireless in their encouragement and support. And then there were others whose generous guidance and counsel I also sought to keep me focused and on the right path.

To all, I want to express my sincere thanks. I hope I have done you proud.

Most of you were friends of mine before this project began, and the rest I now consider as my friends. For that reason I will refer to you by first name only. My true gratitude goes to Wendy, Will, Katie, Carol, John, Avanish, Elay, Ron, Pascal, Mike, Dave x 2, Matt x 3, Jim, Canice, Ken, Gerhard, Bob, Brian, Tim, Kelley, Amanda, Padma, Jill, Mark, Anne, Pat, York, Anne, Walter, Jim, and Peter.

As ever, my family supported me through the ups and down of this effort, and I am forever grateful to Cleona, Robin and Christian for putting up with me.

INDEX

OAK TREE PRESS

Oak Tree Press develops and delivers information, advice and resources for entrepreneurs and managers. It is Ireland's leading business book publisher, with an unrivalled reputation for quality titles across business, management, HR, law, marketing and enterprise topics. NuBooks is its recently-launched imprint, publishing short, focused ebooks for busy entrepreneurs and managers.

In addition, through its founder and managing director, Brian O'Kane, Oak Tree Press occupies a unique position in start-up and small business support in Ireland through its standard-setting titles, as well training courses, mentoring and advisory services.

Oak Tree Press is comfortable across a range of communication media – print, web and training, focusing always on the effective communication of business information.

Oak Tree Press, 19 Rutland Street, Cork, Ireland.
T: + 353 21 4313855 F: + 353 21 4313496.
E: info@oaktreepress.com W: www.oaktreepress.com.

CPSIA information can be obtained at www.ICGtesting.com
Printed in the USA
BVOW03s1632180515

400111BV00009B/10/P